MY SAFE
HAVEN

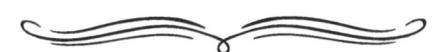

Yavon Smith

All scriptural quotations are from the *King James Version of the Holy Bible*

My Safe Haven

Published by: Yavon Smith

Copyright © 2021 by Yavon Smith

All rights reserved.

Reproduction of text in whole or part without the express written consent by the Authors is not permitted and is unlawful according to the 1976 United States Copyright Act.

Book Production by: Yavon Smith

Printed in the United States of America

No part of this publication may be reproduced, stored in a retrieval system, or transmitted in any form or by any means, electronic, mechanical, photocopying, recording, or otherwise without prior written permission.

Table Of Contents

Introduction..v
Overview...viii
Chapter One - My Birth..1
Chapter Two - The Back House...................................6
Chapter Three - Back Home.......................................11
Chapter Four - Meeting Mama And God...................17
Chapter Five - Discovering The Love Of God............24
Chapter Six - My New Normal...................................27
Chapter Seven - Still That Void..................................31
Chapter Eight - My Breaking Point............................39
Chapter Nine - Music To My Ears..............................43
Chapter Ten - New Home...48
Chapter Eleven - Pent Up Emotions...........................52
Chapter Twelve - Adulthood.......................................62
Chapter Thirteen - How I Overcame My Past............85
Chapter Fourteen - Maturing And Answered Prayers........102
Conclusion - My Hope..112
About the author & contact information...................114

"This is for the Mothers who have had issues raising their children, for the children involved in those issues and for ALL who have (and will) come out of those experiences better..."

God Bless,
Nikki

Introduction

Hello to you, my brother or sister! For years I've said to myself, "I should write a book!" It would be about the things I've experienced in my life, but I never acted on the thought or took it seriously because in my mind, I said, who would want to hear anything about a person's life that they've never met before?

What would I gain by writing my life's story? I guess the real question I should have been asking is, what would God gain if I told my story?

I believe in my heart that God put it in my spirit to author this book. If anything, this could possibly help someone to stand on the word of God or maybe have a different outlook on life while they are in the midst of trying times.

Maybe you are reading this, and you feel that all else has failed and that there's no hope for your life right now.

Maybe you feel the decisions you have made in life have taken you in a direction you just didn't expect it to.

Maybe you are at a place in your life where you are trying to figure out your purpose for existing on the earth, and as a result, you're asking yourself the question, "Where do I go from here?"

Maybe you are having issues with a child(ren) of yours, and you've become overwhelmed; after all, no one gave you a manuscript on how to raise a child; every child is different and has specific needs. So, you pray and do the best you can to rear and teach them what is right.

Maybe you have become familiar with God in your relationship with Him and have become accustomed to prayers like, "Lord, I really need your help getting this job; Lord thank you for a place to live; Lord, I'm ready to get married; Lord, please let me be able to pay for clothes and food for my children…" and you feel those things and those prayers are the only purpose for the relationship you have with God and there is nothing more to do along with those prayers.

Sometimes we can go on in life thinking we have a personal relationship with God, only to discover there is more to having a "personal" relationship with Him than what we thought. Often times we find ourselves dipping and dabbling into the very things He commanded us not to do. He is "A Holy God," one who loves us but requires so much more from us.

Sometimes we believe we know God simply because we asked Him to help give us what we needed, and He answered some of our prayers by His Grace, but it never even occurred to some of us to ask the question.

"Jesus, who am I in you?"

If not careful, we can miss a critical point which is, in this life, it's not just about "us," but about the Kingdom of God and the plan that He has laid out for our lives. It is when the reality of life hits us square in the face that we begin to seriously ask the difficult questions, which is what I had to do.

I had an entire conversation with God in my mind, and I began to ask questions like, "Why does my life seem so unfulfilled? Lord, I know I'm not perfect, and I've made so many mistakes in my life. I know that some of the decisions I've made came with consequences. Some of those consequences I've learned to live with, but Lord, what is the point of living here on earth if I have to deal with feelings of discouragement and frustration continuously? Sometimes I find myself tripping about the way my life has turned out. I don't even understand the point of my existence! **Father, what did I do to deserve all of this drama in my life?** Why am I alive? I don't know the answers to these questions, who I am, let alone who I am in you, Jesus?!"

Everything taking place in my life caused me to ponder on the direction my life was headed. I could not understand the "reason" behind all the craziness that was transpiring around me. So, I went on a journey to discover exactly why my life was going in this direction of unfulfilled purpose and not to a life of **God's perfectly fulfilled purpose** for me.

Upon reading this book, you may come to find that your story isn't exactly like mine, but there may be some similarities. While I will not put every single detail of my story in this book, the point I want to make is this; it is by the Grace of God that I can put something down on paper and no longer have feelings of anger, hurt, rejection, fear, frustration and all of the other destructive, destroying emotions that come with having faced a lot of the challenges I have growing up.

This book is a testimony I never thought would be written. As I said before, all these years, I jokingly said, "I should write a book!" Now, believe me when I tell you, no matter what has happened in your past, in your marriage, with your children, or your relationship with God, as long as you surrender your life to God's "Perfect Will," He is able to help you overcome those things you may believe is impossible. My testimony is your evidence that it is indeed possible.

Overview

I give all honor and glory to God for giving me the strength to endure the fiery trials I have experienced in life. Throughout my childhood years, I learned about Jesus, and I began to build a relationship with Him, believing that He answered prayers. Now, I may not have fully understood what it meant back then to know that God was actually listening to me, but in my innocence, I just believed that God truly existed.

At different stages of my life, I really began to see God for "Who He Is." As I grew older, I continued to develop my relationship with God well into the process of me getting married. My thoughts began to change, and I was now looking at things from a different perspective. I realized that I needed to develop my relationship with God further. Now, I did pray, and those prayers consisted of asking for things or the Lord's help when I needed Him, but I felt my relationship with Him should not only be based on my need for things. I needed to deepen my relationship with Him; I needed to worship Him more and not just with a song but in everyday life.

I needed to communicate with Him more, and of course when you're young, you don't get the full understanding of what your relationship with Him should look like until you begin to grow spiritually and mature in the Word if you take the time to read it and learn of Him of course. That's where spiritual discipline has to come in, and this is how we began to see ourselves in Him. As I began to draw closer through prayer and reading the word of God, I began to see myself take on the characteristics of the fruit of the Spirit I read about in His word. Jesus showed love and compassion for those who sought to be delivered and set free from bondage. He also spoke the truth regarding where our hearts were towards the Father. I saw myself beginning to follow in His footsteps and walking out the purpose He has for me as it was revealed.

I had fallen more in love with Jesus than I thought was ever possible, and today all I can say is, I am in awe of my Heavenly Father! I know Him to be my Father, my Shield, my Buckler, my Protector, and my Provider! I thought I had a relationship with God then, but it was nothing compared to what I know now! I needed to come up higher in Him in order to get to a place where God wanted me to be. My faith in Christ Jesus had to be elevated. For instance, I had to have faith that He would fix my situation even when it looked like it wasn't going to change. I needed faith to trust God in the process and continue to praise Him in the midst of every storm. Having faith in those moments had been a struggle for me. You see, it's a big difference when you're facing a problem that you don't have to see, meaning that the problem isn't directly in front of you. You may have less anxiety about the situation; you can function enough to say, "Oh, I know God can work this out," those types of problems may be on the job or with someone outside of your home. Therefore, you have a break because you don't have to see or deal with them all of the time. You can praise God and believe that a change will happen, but when the problem is directly in front of you, you can't turn a blind eye to it. My faith was being challenged daily because I was living with the problem all day, every day. So, I had to learn to trust God in a way I had not before. I had to learn to pray, praise, and position my way through every challenge that came my way. If not, I wouldn't have been able to withstand those seemly impossible obstacles facing me.

There's a scripture in the Bible that says, "But God hath revealed them unto us by His Spirit: for the Spirit searcheth all things, yea, the deep things of God…" 1 Corinthians 2:10 The more time I spent with God, the more the Holy Spirit illuminated God's Word to me. He continued to reveal those things in me that needed to be finetuned. He was showing me the direction I needed to go and the heart posture I was to have when facing certain obstacles so that I could have peace and learn to still have joy! I can't help but think back to when I was a child; God truly kept me!

Some of you may have heard the scripture John 10:10, which says, "The thief cometh not, but for to steal, and to kill, and to destroy. I am come that they might have life and that they might have it more abundantly." The enemy tried to steal my childhood, but I am still here! I like to make Jeremiah 1:5 personal which says, "Before I (God) formed you (Yavon) in the belly, I knew thee, and before thou camest forth out the womb I sanctified thee, and I ordained thee a prophet unto the nations." This scripture gave me an understanding of what living according to God's plan involves and some of that is suffering; nevertheless, Romans 8:28 says, "And we know that all things work together for good to them that love God, to them who are the called according to His purpose. "Hallelujah!

The enemy tried to steal my joy through events that took place in my past. He tried to destroy my purpose while I was still discovering who I was in Christ Jesus, but oh! Once I understood that I had (and have) a Savior whose name is Jesus, the joy on the inside of me became unexplainable. Unless you have a personal relationship with Him yourself, it is otherwise difficult to explain all of what you feel on the inside. My Savior, Jesus, came to earth and died on the cross to give me (us) abundant life! I later realized that was all I needed to know and believe in order to receive that abundant life He offered me!

Now the enemy knows I have no more time for him and that he is a defeated foe in Jesus' name! The devil literally wants to kill anything that God puts together. Now, when I see Psalms 139:14, which says, "I will praise Thee; for I am fearfully and wonderfully made: marvelous are Thy Works; and that my soul knoweth right well." I can see why the enemy wants to destroy us! Satan is furious because I know who my Savior is. I will continue to praise my Lord Jesus Christ for saving and delivering me out of so many terrible circumstances and obstacles!

So, although the enemy means evil against us, no matter what we face in life, we can believe and know for sure that God is always working things out for our greater good and "His Perfect Plan." Genesis 50:20says, "But as for you, ye thought evil against me: but God meant it unto good, to bring to pass, to save many people alive." Hallelujah!!

In later chapters, you will discover that it took me some time to reach these conclusions. Based upon personal experiences, I've learned a lot of lessons concerning my relationship with God, and I've accepted that He was trying to get my attention because His plans for my life were not what I expected for myself. I am ready to tell my story to all my family, friends, acquaintances, and to those of you I have not met. I want to share how God has been by my side every step of the way.

Please understand that as I begin to put my story together and write this book, I must admit that I am still amazed at how my life has turned out. I found myself grieving and healing at the same time. God has used every stage of my life as a testimony to help me to truly begin to understand His tailormade plan and process for me. He is taking me out of my comfort zone, to shew **(Note: shew in the King James version is God's Revealing, show is the world's reveal)** me how to depend on Him. Even now, it is by faith that I am learning and depending on Him as I write this. Daily I am discovering how to be more like Christ Jesus. I pray that as I tell my story, something in this book will inspire you and that your relationship with God will grow to a level that you've never anticipated. I pray that it will help you get to a place of peace, love, joy, and happiness that is only given and found in Him.

Growing up in a foster home led me to my "Safe Haven," which is my church home. Looking back, I cannot help but think and say, "Wow, Lord! Your hand really was on my life!" Although I still don't have all the answers concerning the rest of my life, I can now say for "myself" without a shadow of a doubt, when you have not been raised up in a Godly home from the beginning, it is hard to see how God was with you. Now, looking back in hindsight, I can see how the Lord may have protected me from some situations that could have gone much worse than what I experienced. However, it was enough for me to know, as I stated before, that God truly existed! May I put *extra emphasis* when I make this statement? Now, I know with every fiber of my being that My God was with me! Glory be to God!

Let me give you some background on my earlier life, growing up. My mother would constantly tell the story of how I was conceived and how she went into labor with me. How one day she was about to take her last hit of drugs before the Lord put into her remembrance that He loved her and that if she would just give her problems to Him, He would save her. When I was younger, I used to get so annoyed with her telling this story over and over repeatedly, but it's also my testimony as well. Now I understand why she tells this story everywhere she goes to whoever will listen. After all, the Lord did save her! Glory be to God!!

So, with that being said, my brother or sister, I will start from the very beginning, when I entered into this world but let me end this chapter with a prayer to acknowledge and thank my God.

Dear Heavenly Father,

I want to thank you for your love and kindness. You are my God; you have filled my heart with so much joy. You have shown me that you will never leave me nor forsake me as your Word stated. I've read your Word intellectually, and I understand what it means, but it has become very clear in my mind and heart how much you love to perform your "Promises." I know that you want to bring your promises to pass for all of your children reading this book. I know that you want to heal broken-hearted as you have healed mine. I know that you want the best for them, just like you do for me. I thank you that you love me enough to chasten me. Lord, I thank you for pulling me out of a place of despair and bringing me into a place of wholeness. Today, I know for a fact that if I didn't have you in my life, I would not be here right now at this very place with you. I love you, Lord; I honor you, my King, and praise you, my Father.

In Jesus' name, I pray, Amen!

Chapter One
My Birth

I was supposed to come into the world on March 25, 1976, but because of my mother's bad habits (drinking, smoking, hanging out late hours, and partying...), I was born three months early. My mother shared that in December of 1975, her water did not completely break, but it started leaking. She went to the hospital and was told I would not live because it was too early for her water to break, and I was not fully formed. The doctors wanted my mother to let them take me. They believed that if they did not take me right then, she and I would die.

As my mother lay there in the hospital watching the machine that monitored my heartbeat, thoughts came to her mind that she didn't know for sure if they were her own or if God influenced them. Nevertheless, she wondered if she would always wonder if she had held onto this baby (me) would it have lived? Well, she decided at that moment that she was going to take the risk and continue carrying me to see if I would live. My mother said all she knew was that she couldn't care more about herself than this child.

She knew that it was God in the form of the Holy Spirit doing His Perfect Will and Work! Now, mind you, there was so much drama getting me here, it almost sounds comical to me when I hear about it now, but it truly showed me how there was a battle with the forces of darkness to get me into this world. I can't help but wonder what God was up to and what the enemy was trying to stop?!

Before all of this took place, my mother had already tried to abort me in all kinds of ways you could imagine, but God would not allow it. So, here it is now, the doctors are trying to get rid of me. They thought they were making the best decision for their patient. One doctor got so angry with my mother, she called her foolish and a few other choice words, all because my mother told her that she was going to see if she was woman enough to hold this child, and that was THAT! The doctor sent her home, telling her to stay on bed rest and only get up to use the restroom to buy time for me to develop fully.

On January 1, 1976, my mother began having excruciating pains, and my father rushed her to the hospital. As they were in route, they got pulled over by the police. The policeman asked him why was he speeding? My father told the policeman that my mother was in labor. The policeman said, "She doesn't look pregnant to me!" At that time, my mother wasn't noticeably large in the belly since I wasn't a full-term baby. My mother had to pull up her blouse and show this stranger the leaking water between her legs. At that point, the friendly officer drove ahead of them to ensure they got to the hospital. When my mother tells her story, she says she sees how special I was and am to God. She says, "God sent you an escort to be born!"

Immediately upon arrival, my mother was rushed into the delivery room. While the nurses were preparing her for delivery, she looked down and noticed a little yellow bag. It was her water bag with not enough water in it to be broken. She said it looked like a water balloon had fallen out of her, and because I was so small, she was in labor for a long while. She said I was too weak to push myself out.

Once I arrived, all the nurses and doctors began to immerse themselves in working on me immediately. I weighed two pounds and two ounces and quickly went down to one pound and thirteen ounces. According to my father, I looked like a jellyfish and a little rat in his large palms. I remember he and my mother sharing with me that before I was transported to another hospital, a line full of their friends and other people they didn't know were looking across the nursery window trying to get a glimpse of this tiny baby. After all, this was New Year's Day. The doctors and staff had witnessed a miracle baby! **Glory be to God!**

I don't think I ever thought of this before, but something tells me that there is meaning in that alone. The hospital had a helicopter waiting and was ready to take me to the nearest Children's Hospital. My mother stated, "God has a flying chariot for this one." While at the Children's Hospital, the doctor said to my mother, "Your baby girl has not developed enough; she isn't going to make it past two hours. If she does live, she will be blind, deaf, and retarded," **But God! He had a plan!**

My mother said all she knew was that prayer came out of her mouth; she knew it was not her praying; she didn't know how to pray, nor did she know how to use the words that were being prayed out of her mouth! I was in the incubator for about two months with patches on my eyes. I had all kinds of tubes, cords, and wires attached to me from head to toe. The doctors told her that the incubator had cooked the retina in my eyes. Therefore, I would be blind and would never be able to hear. All kinds of things were told to her that would be wrong with me, and because of my father's "situation," she decided to put me up for adoption.

Weeks had gone by, and now it was the day before my mother was to sign the adoption papers. She went to the hospital to see me for what she thought would be the last time. You see, she had never been able to hold me except through the gloves in the incubator, so she didn't have a connection or a bond with me the way she would have had she gotten the chance to feel, touch, and kiss me like other mothers.

As soon as she walked in, the nurse asked her, "Mother, would you like to hold your baby?" She sat down, and they put **Yavon Nichol Alexander** in her arms, and from that moment on, she knew that she could not give her baby away. The following day, she was due to sign the adoption papers, but suddenly she had a change of heart, and she told them, "NO! I can't do this!" A week later, all four pounds and five ounces of me went home with my mother and siblings.

Now, this is a funny story! My mother once told me that I was so small, she would have to carry me around on a pillow. Can you imagine how tiny I must have looked, being that she is over six feet tall?! What makes this even funnier is, my mother was taller than my daddy, so he wore shoes with thick soles to make himself appear taller so he could at least try and reach her height. Lol

One time my mother told me that she had taken me outside, and a man thought she was forcing me to walk, and he became upset. Lol She explained to him that it was all right because I was older than what I looked. I was maybe a year old, but I was tiny for my age.

I don't think I ever realized how this part of my life's story was important. As I said before, I used to get so annoyed when my mother would tell this story over and over again. God knew that at some point this would be my testimony as well. I don't know who this story will bless, but one thing I do know for sure is that God will get the Glory out of this story!

Not only was I conceived out of wedlock, but my father was already married to another woman who I will speak on later in this book. I will tell you how this courageous mother and woman of God played a huge role in parts of my life, and to think that all of this is no surprise to God! Even I have tripped off some of the things that have happened to me! My story reminds me of the situations that some went through in the Bible, like Abraham (Father of a multitude), Joshua (Savior), Joseph (Increase), Moses (Drawn out), and his sister Mariam (Tear), just to name a few. When I truly started looking at my life and what I have been through, it began to form in my mind that there was and is something more to my life than what I can even articulate.

Chapter Two

The Back House

I can remember as far back as five years old, but I don't remember much before then. I remember riding a blue car with my mother and her guy friend. We were driving and then we stopped. I had no clue this would turn out to be the beginning of some of the most traumatic experiences in my childhood.

We got out of the car and walked to the back of the house. My mother began to knock on the door; no one was home. I remember waiting for a moment to see if someone would arrive at some point but still, no one showed up. We went to the front of the house, I guess, to see if anyone was outside, but no one was hanging out because it was the middle of the week and not the weekend. Nobody hung out on a weekday. So, we went back to the back of the house, and my mother told me to sit down on the porch while she went back to the car to get my clothes, which were in plastic bags, and she sat them on the porch. I remember thinking to myself, this sure looks like a lot of bags. It didn't look like I would be staying there for just a couple of days. Just then, my mother told me to wait where I was sitting and that she'd be back. I saw her walk out towards the front and disappear, not knowing that it would be a long while before I would ever see her again.

In my young mind, I had no understanding of what was going on. It never crossed my mind that my mommy was leaving me there to live. So, I sat there and waited like an obedient child. Still, no one showed up. I don't remember exactly how long I sat there; I just remember the sun starting to come down a little. Eventually, I went out to the front to see if anybody was out there. No one was there, not even my mommy. I cried and cried, and no one heard me. I don't know how long it was that I stood out there. At some point, I saw a police car pulling up to me. The officer asked, "Who is your mommy? Do you know where she is?" All I remember doing was crying; I couldn't speak.

The police put me in the front seat with them while trying to console me as best as they could. They took me to a woman's home, and other children were there. It seemed like I was there for at least a day or two, crying for my mommy all night. I don't even recall if I ever slept. I can remember being on the edge of the bed, crying my eyes out. When the police finally found my mother, I remember being happy to see her. I remember her taking me to the shoe store. I got some green high-top converse vans. I smiled because I was back with her again, but that would only last for so long. I soon realized that I was not going home with her; she took me right back to the house whose porch she left me on. This time someone would be home. These people were supposedly my "Godparents." They were an older couple who had children older than me, and they were always fighting.

This was just the beginning stages of my childhood. My life as a child was about to be filled with many twists and turns. All I can say is, **"Glory be to God!"** I'm telling you, my brother or sister, if it had not been for my Lord and Savior keeping me intact throughout all these trials and tribulations, I just don't know how life would be for me right now! It is only by the Grace, Mercy, and Love of God that I'm still here. The enemy had already failed at his attempts in stopping me from getting here, now here he was again, trying to destroy the early stages of my childhood, but my God was my Protector!

I may have lived with these people for close to three years, and so much had happened to me, but I only remember certain events that took place. I was sexually abused at the age of six by her husband, who was a huge man. He was an alcoholic and a pervert. His wife would either be in bed asleep or at the front of the house watching television. It would be those times that he would sneakily pull me into my room, lay me down on the bed, and try to have his way with me. Considering that I was so small, there was only so much he could do to me without me screaming at the top of my lungs and him getting caught. His son was not far from him. He would always try to lure me down into the basement of their house to have his wicked way with me. The first time he tried to force me to do things to him that no child should ever encounter, but I would somehow manage to escape him.

One day we went to the beach. I don't know if you ever saw those BBQ pits that were deep into the sand? Well, this was back in the early eighties. I happened to wander off to the area where the BBQ pit was to play. I decided to walk around the edge of the circular pit, not knowing that the coals were still burning with fire. I jumped into those hot coals like it was nobody's business! The pit was so deep, and mind you; I was already a small child. I can't remember if I screamed to get someone's attention or if I managed to pull myself out of the pit!

Eventually, somebody came to my rescue, but by that time, the skin on both my feet began to form into a humongous blister. That ruined whatever fun we had left. I was rushed to the hospital. The trip to the hospital was excruciating for everybody. The husband and wife got into an argument again; he was driving too slowly; maybe he was too drunk to drive. He was one of those people who would get so drunk that his eyes would turn bloodshot red. Imagine a dark-skinned man with bloodshot red eyes; he would look scary as I don't know what!! His wife was already upset over the turn of events. She told him to pull over; she got out of the car and began to walk while carrying me over her shoulder as I cried hysterically. He continued driving alongside us, begging her to get back into the car. It was a bit much, and I was in so much pain! I'm not even sure how long it took us to get to the hospital, but it wasn't long before I was sent into a room for them to attend to both of my feet. To this day, I still have the scars as a reminder.

I remember another time we went on a long road trip. I think we were going out of the state into a country somewhere to visit the wife's mother and family. It took us several days to get to our destination. It was hot and sticky; riding in that station wagon was no joke at that time! We stopped to rest and have lunch in an area that looked deserted. Somehow, I found myself sinking and couldn't understand what was happening. I realized later that I had stepped into some quicksand! I tried to get myself out, but I began to sink quickly! Lord knows I was screaming for my life! By the time someone saw me, I was deep down into the quicksand up to my chest area. Someone quickly began to pull on me hard, but I wasn't coming up fast enough. If I remember correctly, they also had to use the car we drove in to help pull me out!

I'm telling you, my brother or sister, I had only been living about six years, and already there were so many attempts on my life. Even as I am putting this story together, you can clearly see that God has been protecting me from the hands of the enemy all this time! To some on the outside, it would have seemed as if I were living a normal life. As I sit back and think about this family, I know and realize that I had been placed in an extremely broken home. Everyone had their own demons to fight. One daughter ran away. Another daughter got pregnant at a young age. One son was shot and killed, while another son went to jail. This family did not understand that the enemy roamed to and fro to seek whom he may devour. (**1 Peter 5:8**) They did not have the knowledge or discernment to know that the enemy was out to destroy me, a child of the King. It wasn't until years later that I understood how dysfunctional life around me really was.

Chapter Three

Back Home

I was about seven or eight years old when I was told that I would be moving back with my mother and two older sisters. I had three sisters, but one of them lived with her father. I was so excited to be going home to my own family! I was grinning from ear to ear! I finally got to my mother's place, and I saw one of my sisters. I jumped on her with so much excitement! My other sister had not made it home yet, but I hugged her so tight when she did! I was so talkative back then. I sat between my oldest sister's legs while we watched tv, talked, and laughed. There was so much joy coming from them! I tell you, the love they had for me was so genuine, it didn't matter how far away we were from one another!

They let it be known to everyone in the neighborhood too! I am talking about their friends and even their boyfriends too, Lol (laugh out loud) it did not matter! Everyone knew about their baby sister. They would tell you that I was their baby instead of my mother's baby. This was the first Christmas we were back together; my oldest sister took me shopping at a toy store called Toys 'R' Us and let me pick out every toy I wanted! By the time I was done, my things had filled two whole baskets! We went home, and she wrapped my gifts. She bought the biggest tree and put all the presents underneath it. On Christmas day, I woke up early to open my presents. To her surprise, I remembered and knew what every gift was before I opened it; she was so tickled by that. This was a moment that I cherished in my heart.

Now you all probably know how popular Michael Jackson was back in the eighties. Well, I used to love me some Michael Jackson! Lol, I had the red leather jacket (so I thought) with the zippers, earrings, gloves, socks, the t-shirt, and shoes! I used to try and moonwalk on our kitchen floor! I believe I was the life of the party in my family! Lol, I guess when you are around genuine love, you can truly be free to smile and be a real kid! Unfortunately for me, it would only last for so long.

I started attending school across the street from my house and was bullied. I had my first fight trying to defend myself from these tall girls. I may have gotten punched, but that didn't stop me from attempting to get a punch in for myself! I don't know why, but I happened to be that little girl they wanted to push around, and it just may have been due to jealousy; I don't know for sure. Another time, one of those girls had her friends or family rough me up. I remember running home and telling my older sisters. My big sisters were so upset, they marched themselves over to their house, and before I knew it, there was a fight among all the girls! I don't know how many there were, but it took a few people to break up the fight before it stopped.

It was crazy! The beef between my sisters and those girls lasted for an exceptionally long time. Every time they saw one another, it was a fight. My sisters did not play when it came to their little sister!

I believe during that time; my mother worked at a nightclub. I always heard about this club that she and all her friends attended. This was "THE" spot where everybody hung out, and everyone knew each other. My mother worked and partied all of the time. She was working and having fun, well, at least that's what it looked like to me. They were having the time of their lives. She had lots of friends, and every one of them knew about her miracle baby! Sometimes it was interesting to watch her be the life of the party. She would have guests over; I would listen to them play records and join in on the fun until she would make me go to bed.

One late night, my mother took me to this deserted park, and she did something she had never done before. She climbed on one of the swings and put me on top of her lap, facing her. We began to swing up and down, back and forth. We had so much fun. All of a sudden we began laughing and I cannot tell you what was so funny for the life of me! I think we were just being silly, but we would burst out laughing so hard for what seemed like hours while swinging up and down. My mother had this laughter that would have you cracking up so hard, although no one told a joke! Lol, I'm not exactly sure why this particular night was special to me. It wasn't until years later that I realized I was going to need this memory of us because it would remind me of the mother I had before life would take us on a journey that would eventually lead us to the path we did not see coming. To this day, the memories of my mother's infectious laughter that could brighten up your day is what I will always remember and hold dear to my heart.

As time went on, my mother's personality became unusual in ways that I had never seen before. She was acting in a manner that was so unlike the mother I knew her to be. Let me pause right here for a second, my brother or sister. As I tell my story, please keep in mind that what I'm about to share happened many years ago. I am sharing this part of my story because this was part of the root that trickled down through my life growing up. It is a significant part of my story that required a lot of healing and forgiveness. I would like you to read and understand from a spiritual perspective. The things in the past that occurred with my mother were before she gave her life over to Jesus. The way I see it, it was the **"GRACE"** of God operating in her life, but what you don't know before Christ can also have the potential of hurting you and others in the long run.

Continuing on, my mother and one of my sisters would get into these huge blowout fights. One night, it was so bad that the police had to come out and investigate. My sister was laid out in the floor with a pool stick lying next to her. I was very young, and I wasn't sure why they were fighting or what caused the conflict between the two. All I know is my sister was on the hallway floor with a pool of blood surrounding her head. I remember the fear I felt seeing her cry while in so much pain. Eventually, someone put me in one of the bedrooms to keep me from seeing her in the condition she was in. Honestly, I don't think my mother was in her right frame of mind. She was so upset, and so was I! I was crying hysterically, which made matters worse. I believe I must have said something in defense of my sister, which angered my mother.

That anger triggered her to knock me upside my head causing me to hit the bed rail. It was such a hard blow! I still have the scar today. There were times my cousins and their friends would visit us. Usually, I'd be the youngest in the group, and the older kids were supposed to "keep their eyes on me." We spent a lot of nights together while our mothers were out partying on the weekends. We lived in a small space; four or five of us would be sleeping in the same bed. One time I felt someone touch me inappropriately. The room was so dark I couldn't tell who was doing their dirty deeds. I started crying, and one of my sisters grabbed me and put me next to her until I was able to go back to sleep. I never said a word.

The LORD (All capital letters is the Father) God (Uppercase G, lowercase 'od' = Jesus- Philippians 2:11) was my protector even though I did not know Him yet!

I did not know He even existed at that time. If somebody would have told me that He answers prayers, maybe, just maybe, He would have spared us all that heartache of a very dysfunctional family life. Now, I do remember going to church once or twice, but I didn't understand anything about God or His son Jesus at that time. Unfortunately, we didn't have a foundation in Christ; therefore, life for us went further downhill.

My older sister wasn't home very often, and my other sister got pregnant when she was around fifteen or sixteen. No one really knew it until it was time for her to deliver my niece. She was so precious! I remember saving my lunch ticket from school because it matched her birth date, and I put it in her crib. I remember watching her sleep so peacefully. She was a fresh breath of air, but it wasn't long after that before we would have to up and move again. This time it would just be my mother and I living together and not my two older sisters. Every once in a blue moon, I would spend the weekend with my other sister at her father's and stepmothers' house. They would take me to their church. I got baptized at the age of seven, and even though I did not know Jesus at the time, I did accept Him as my personal Savior. So, I thank God for my sister's stepmother opening her heart to me. The Lord knew that she would be a willing vessel to help start me on my journey to understand who Jesus Christ is.

My mother and I was now living in an apartment and I was seeing my father. According to my mother, my daddy was always in my life. He would take me to my grandparents' home. Everybody in the town knew about me except his wife. He did not want his wife to know what he had been up to. I vaguely remember being around my two older brothers before meeting his wife. Meanwhile, my mama (mama is my daddy's wife) found out about me through a neighbor, and according to her, she didn't want to believe it. Those neighbors sure were some investigators! They would take pictures of my dad taking me and some other children (I think they were my sisters) in their home. He took care of my sisters whenever he had the opportunity. Everyone knew my daddy had a heart for kids and those who sincerely needed help.

Eventually, my daddy had to come clean and tell mama about me before somebody else told her. It was a little late; she already knew about me, although she never shared this with my daddy. Mama stated that she was upset about this at first. Then she told him that if he wanted to be a part of his daughters' life, she would not keep him away from me. I was not responsible for anything that he and my mother did. I was the innocent one in this. She said she would love me just as if she would love her own kids.

Chapter Four

Meeting Mama And God...

My daddy experienced a life-changing event, and it was a wake-up call for him. One morning mama (my daddy's wife) had gotten up about 5:30 a.m.; she was sitting on the side of her bed, still trying to gather herself to wake up fully, she had been up maybe about 5 to 10 minutes when suddenly she felt her bed making jerking movements. She turned around to see that my daddy was having a seizure. With her being a nurse, she knew what precautions to take to give him the help he needed at that moment. She went over to him to ensure that his head was turned to the side so he wouldn't choke. After about 3 minutes, he stopped seizing, but she could see that he was beginning to turn cyanotic, meaning that he was turning blue. When that happens, something is cutting off the person's airway.

My dad's mouth was wide open, so she could see that his tongue was blocking his airway. She ran to the kitchen and grabbed a spoon so she could move his tongue. As she was doing this, she managed to yell out to my nine-year-old brother, who was still sleeping at the time in the other room. Mama told him to call 911 and come into the room with her. My brother held the phone up to my mama's mouth so she could speak with the operator while attending to my daddy. He had seized a couple more times before the paramedics arrived at the house, which was less than 5 minutes after she called. My daddy was rushed to the nearest hospital, and upon arrival, they ran a CT scan and MRI of his brain and found that he had a brain tumor and needed surgery immediately. Thankfully, the surgery was successful, but it was the beginning of a reality check for my dad!

You see, during the early years of his life, my dad was living the way he saw fit. He was a good-looking man, very friendly, and had an outgoing personality. He had a way with people; everyone he encountered tended to gravitate towards him. Some would say my daddy was a fighter on the streets and would throw down every chance he got. If my mother tells it, she and my daddy fought for ten years over me. They went to court, and he tried to get out of paying child support by changing his identity, name, and social security number. It was so much drama that took place, but it's almost hard to believe that these very same people went through all of this! My daddy's life totally changed after the brain surgery.

Although I didn't know Christ as I know Him now, I still believe that even with all that we endured as a family, God was still in the midst, orchestrating our lives! It's truly a testimony to how much God (God is love." 1JOHN 4:8) truly loves my father, "both" my mother's and myself! The Lord used each of them and their situations to show me that His Love is Perfect and Everlasting despite our choices!

"We love Him because He first loved us." 1 John 4:19

After the surgery, my parents had a heart-to-heart talk about me coming to stay with my father on the weekends. It was about this time that I would meet my stepmother for the first time. You can probably tell by now that I consider my father's wife my mother as well. For the sake of clarity, I've been referring to my father's wife as "Mama" and my mother as "Mother," so you'll know the difference. Continuing on, I was nine years old at this time and what's funny is I still remember what I was wearing and how I looked. I had on a red two-piece dress; it had some type of black print on them. The dress was paired with thick black tights and shiny patent leather shoes. I'm sure my hair was in a ponytail. Lol Thinking back on it, all I can do is laugh. The reason being is, I felt the outfit looked crazy on me! Just imagine, I'm a tall skinny girl wearing a whole suit just to meet mama for the first time!

I was at daddy's house waiting for mama to come home from work so I could meet her. The moment had come, and she walked through the front door in her nursing uniform. Mama went straight into the kitchen. If I remember correctly, she began to prepare dinner. She started cutting up some chicken and seasoning it. I went and stood right beside her at the sink and said, "Hello, how was your day today?" She said, "My day went well; how was your day?" Mama began to tell me that she was glad to meet me and had heard so much about me. Our first conversation was very cordial. I went and sat in a chair by the kitchen door in the hallway and watched her cook as we continued to converse. Mama's first impression of me was that she was cute and soft-spoken, but that was because I didn't know her well. My first impression of mama was she's nice. My mama is a strong woman; she chose to accept me into her family. Given the circumstances, she still loved me, and that wasn't anything but the Grace of God! He gave her the strength to love me just as if she had given birth to me.

Later on, I would meet my aunties, uncles, and a whole lot of cousins. One of my cousins and I are the same age. We clicked very well and were almost inseparable growing up, but

I was just as close to my older cousins as well. The rest of my family also showed their love for me. Well not everyone. Lol, Sometimes you'll find that one person who feels "some type of way towards you." Trust me, even at a young age; you can detect when a family member isn't fond of you or is even jealous. Some of them tried to hide their feelings, and I have even pretended as if I didn't notice. I never fully understood what it was that bothered them about me. I've always been "different," so it could have been a combination of things. Maybe there were some insecurities they had within themselves unbeknownst to me that were never dealt with.

Despite all of the ups and downs that came with my family, I felt there was more love among us to spread around. The others, well, just picked and chose what days they felt like they wanted to like or love me, but honestly, I felt like the situation I was in now was way better than the one I was in before. Later I'll share what I went through in my teenage years, and you'll see why I made this particular statement. God knows exactly who and what we will need even when we cannot see or understand it in our "natural" minds. God put me in and around a family that was one of the most incredible groups of people one could ever hope to be around. That was what I needed at that time. It was God's way of showing me "His Love" through this family…my family.

I was now visiting daddy and mama but still living with my mother in an apartment. A lady who lived next door to us worked for the school I was enrolled in. I only mention this because it's essential to my story. You see, this same neighbor came over to our place and asked my mother if she could take me to church with her. My mother said yes, and I remember getting dressed. I wore that same old red and black dress I wore when I first met mama, you know, with the black tights and patent leather shoes and went right on to church with her and her grandchildren. This nice lady took me to church again that following Sunday. That was the day I felt I had heard the Holy Ghost and felt Him tugging at my heart.

I remember precisely where I was sitting and what the Lord had spoken. The Pastor and founder of the church had preached such a powerful message. When he finished preaching, he asked if anyone wanted to join the church and accept Jesus Christ as their personal Savior. I remember sitting there, and in my Spirit, I felt that tug; there was a pull in me to get up and join. Then I heard God say very clearly in my heart, "If you go, I will save your mother." It was as if I was being led to the front; I don't even remember how I made it to the front of the church, but what I did know is I felt led to join this church, the place I would call my **"Safe Haven."**

Later that afternoon, we went back to a musical service that the church was having, and to my surprise, they ushered me right onto the choir stand with the other children! I didn't know one lyric to the songs they were singing; I just rocked to the music as I was instructed to. It was as if I belonged! What I want you to understand is that God sees and knows all. You see, the night before I joined this church, my mother got in this huge fight with a guy friend of hers, and their loud screaming match had awakened me. I guess my mother wanted relief and to escape the reality of her life at that moment. Later that night, she went into our kitchen, but she never turned the light on. At that moment, she didn't realize I was sitting on the edge of the couch watching her through the reflection of the refrigerator as she got high.

I didn't know what she was doing at that time, but I could sense that it was wrong. I prayed to God and asked that He would help my mother. That's why this part of my testimony is so important. The third time I went to church, my mother had come to the church only to pick me up early; she claimed that she was taking me to Disneyland. Well, we never made it. This was the beginning of God's plan taking effect in my life. The enemy was working overtime to keep me from attending this church, my "Safe Haven." I realized later that God is always ahead of Satan!! For the next couple of weeks, I did not attend church, and that life was about to bring more challenging experiences.

I was about nine years old during the time my mother and I went to visit her friend; I'll refer to her as "Lady J." Her friend had no idea that our visit would not only affect my life but hers as well. My mother and Lady J sat and conversed for what seemed like hours until my mother got up. I must have sensed something was off as she started to move because I got up immediately and tried to follow her right out the front door. We stood on the porch together, and I felt a familiar feeling at that exact moment. It was the same feelings I had felt when I was five, which was ABANDONMENT!!! I felt it in the pit of my stomach. HURT!! I felt that wound opening back up. DISAPPOINTMENT!!! I was about to be left AGAIN and with another stranger!!! I didn't know Lady J personally or if I could trust her. Man! I thought all this pain had gone away! To be honest, my brother or sister, at that time, I didn't understand those "emotions" or how to define them. I didn't know that I was not healed from the previous deeds that happened to me in the first place.

At this point, all of my unrecognizable emotions remained hidden, bottled up, and were never released at that moment because neither my mother nor father knew all of what happened to me years prior. Secondly, I didn't know I could release those secrets I carried or express how I felt. I stood there looking into my mother's eyes for answers, but I couldn't say a word. I could not articulate to her what I was feeling; then, she said, "I'm coming back for you tomorrow." But tomorrow never came.

Chapter Five

Discovering The Love Of God

Weeks had gone by, and I was now attending another school. My mother made an agreement with Lady J for her to keep me. I guess one would think I should have gotten used to moving from place to place, and I never did. During this time, my mother received a county check to help pay for food and other essentials. Part of the agreement was to divide the check among the two of them so that Lady J could help provide for my basic needs. Ultimately, Lady J ended up receiving her own check to provide for me. It wasn't the situation I was hoping for but I thought to myself, at least this time I have my own room.

What I didn't know was that Lady J and my mother had been friends for close to twenty years before I was born. I thought I was seeing her for the first time at the age of nine, but Lady J had been in my life all this time. It turns out there was a whole lot of history behind these two ladies that I was not aware of. So far, every person my mom entrusted me to wasn't so trustworthy.

I did have something I felt was divine happen to me during the whole ordeal. Sometime later, Lady J and I, along with a friend of hers, attended the church I had joined (My Safe Haven)! It happened to be within walking distance from Lady J's house! Who could have known?! I was now close to a church that would help mold and shape me into the woman I would become. I am telling you, my brother or sister, this could only be the work of the one true omniscient (All-Knowing) God!

Although things were not perfect, I would at least have stability for the next six years due to my new living arrangements. Since I was now considered a foster child, I would have to put up with visits from the Department of Children and Family Services (D.C.F.S) on a regular basis. Every time they came, the house had to be intact, meaning everything needed to be cleaned and in its place. I not only needed to look like I was well kept, but there couldn't be any signs of abnormal behavior, so I never said a word even though things were not always "ok" being in the custody of Lady J. Not only did I intentionally hide what was taking place in the home from D.C.F.S, but I had also already developed a tendency of hiding how I truly felt, which made it easier to pretend that all was well. Now, in the beginning, things were not as bad, and that may have been because our relationship was "new," but as time went on, different instances would occur.

For example, I found myself getting into trouble for things I did that most would probably consider normal. I would be scolded for doing something I thought I didn't need permission to do, like getting a snack to eat. I understand that every individual has their own way of disciplining children, but at some point, I felt things had gotten out of hand, but I continued to stay quiet. Why? I only continued dealing with the issues at "home" with Lady J because I wanted to keep attending my church home. That was what I cared about the most. I loved being at my "Safe Haven"! It was the only house that truly felt like home. If I had told the D.C.S.F that anything was wrong, they would investigate, and if necessary, they would remove me out of the house and place me into another. So, I decided that I would make it seem as if I was in the safest place I could be, even if that wasn't the case. On top of things not being so great at home, I was getting bullied at school almost every other day, but I was determined that I would endure it all so I could stay at my church, "My Safe Haven."

My brother or sister, please understand where I'm coming from and why I made this decision. This was an extremely critical time in my life, maybe more than the beginning of my childhood. In my Safe Haven, I discovered God really existed and began to develop a relationship with Him, and might I add that this church was on fire! I don't mean it was literally in flames, nor am I only referring to when we would shout and speak in tongues as the Holy Ghost would move. There was a demonstration of the "fruits" of God's Spirit as well! The Spirit of love was in this church! The Spirit of peace and unity was in this church! At least, that's what I felt during that time. That's why I called it my "Safe Haven"!

There were some very influential people who played key roles in my life as it pertained to helping me to develop my relationship with Christ and gaining confidence. I truly gained protectors, mentors, teachers, and wise counselors. I grew into my adolescent years, and I desired to know more about Christ. I couldn't see or physically touch God, but His love was demonstrated through those persons, and I came to learn more about Him. Jesus became more real to me, and it was easy for me to gravitate towards these loving people, even after all I had been through. It was something special about the way they cared not only for me but also for the other kids at this church.

I truly felt Loved…

Chapter Six

My New Normal

Years had passed while living with Lady J, and the church remained a significant part of my life. Every Sunday morning, I'd wake up, shower, get dressed, and walk to church. I would be there at eight in the morning and stay until whatever time church ended. Oftentimes this wouldn't be until well after 9 pm. It was my second home. We had Sunday School, Junior Church, Friday Night Live, and Candlelight Services. You name it; I was there! Choir rehearsal would be all night on Fridays, and then we'd have usher board practice early Saturday mornings. No wonder I felt like I lived at church! Lol Church was all I knew back then.

I loved attending the Friday Night Live services; there would be competitions between the youth and young adult choir. One of the youths would pick an adult in the church to imitate and vice versa. Everybody knew who you were imitating, which was hilarious; it made the services so much fun! The point of this particular service was to understand that you were being watched whether you realized it or not. It was to demonstrate how you conducted yourself in church and shed light on how you worshiped God with your life.

During that time, choirs were extremely popular, and there was a song called "Genesis" that our youth choir was well known for singing around town. We were asked to perform that song at many different churches all over the city, but it wasn't just the song they loved to hear. Our choir director would throw down when it came to directing that song! Now don't get me wrong, I'm not playing down our young adult choir, and Lord knows I wanted to be in the young adult choir so bad. I couldn't wait to turn eighteen because that's the age you had to be to join. One of my fondest memories of the choir was the musicals that were arranged.

The ladies would wear these huge collard, long, fuchsia-colored dresses that would reach their knees. The men wore black pants and white shirts with a fuchsia bow tie. As the service proceeded, without making the church aware of what they were doing, each choir member would discreetly come in at different times one by one and sit down at the edge of the pew. When it came time for the processional of the choir, there was a domino effect in their starting. They would each stand up and start singing in the order of tenor, alto, and soprano, ***"No, I'll never stop praising the Lord, No, I'll never stop praising the Lord…."*** Then they would go into the middle of the aisle and begin to form a line that crisscrossed as they walked down to the choir stand, demonstrating God's awesomeness.

Some people loved the performance, and that was all they cared to see, but for me, it was the understanding of God's creation. My desire to sing with the choir was not for popularity nor was it about performing a song. Every word that was sung had meaning to it, and I believe that many of the choir members believed in their hearts what they were singing. It's too bad I don't have the gift of singing. Lol, These songs really helped me learn more about God. Most of the lyrics to the songs were inspired by scriptures. Back then it was common for the chosen lead's testimony to mirror the lyrics of the song and because of this, there was passion behind the words they sang. The testimonies, along with the melody of the song, glorified God and made Jesus more real to me!

During a musical program, I decided to record the choir on one of those eighties retro red radio cassette recorder boom boxes. Do you know the program hadn't even started, but they began singing, "We're going to make it, we're going to make it, just be sure that you keep holding on"? They sang that song for over an hour, and each of them began testifying! Many shared how good God had been to them and how He brought them out of a fiery trial or test. During these times, I began to understand that the God they served was the same God that was helping me through the hard times I was having at home with Lady J; and every time I heard the young adults sing, it was like hearing the sounds of heaven. I believed every word they sang; those words seemed to surround me and made me feel as if I was in a safe place.

Lady J didn't know all I had endured during my earlier years before I was placed with her. Nor did she realize how her actions affected me during that time and later on in life. If you were to ask me if Lady J loved me back then, I would have flat out told you, NO! Did she care for me? I believe she did, in her own way, but Lady J didn't have any children of her own, so maybe that made it hard for her to love someone else's child, especially when they were just sprung on you. Now, on the other hand, I do feel that if you like children, you will treat them with love and kindness no matter if you gave birth to them or not. Now please understand, Lady J's personality is NOWHERE near the same now as it was all those years ago, and even then, she still had some funny and perky ways about her.

Hopefully, this makes what I'm about to share with you a little less difficult for you to read as I share my story. With the help and strength of the Lord, I was able to forgive her for the things that took place. There were quite a few things that happened, but I will give you an idea of how I felt and what I went through while living with Lady J. There are also some key factors I want to point out so you can understand the importance of FORGIVENESS.

I loved my "Safe Haven" I would love to have lived there because I dreaded going back home. One of the reasons had to do with the strict rules I had to abide by. Other reasons I didn't care to stay there was due to boredom, feeling lonely, and being plain ole sick and tired of being a punching bag. During those times, I would be on my knees praying and crying to God every night, asking Him to save my mother and to let her come back to get me so that we could be a family again. Maybe it was going to be better than before. At least that's what I was hoping for. I would also ask God, "Why am I always getting into trouble for something so stupid?" Yes, there were times I played a part in getting into trouble, but these were the kind of conversations I would have with God. Some nights my prayers were in the form of tears due to so much hurt and pain because I just didn't get it.

Chapter Seven

Still That Void...

As I got older, things became increasingly intense between Lady J and I. One day I was at home by myself; Lady J had not come home from work yet. I was hungry and wanted something to snack on. I saw some buttery club crackers on top of the refrigerator. I never had them before, and I decided to try them out. I was so hungry that I ended up eating a good amount of them and putting what was left back into the box. Those crackers were so good! Lol, I didn't know I wasn't supposed to eat them without Lady J's permission. Honestly, I don't know if I got in trouble because I didn't ask or if I ate too many of them. When she got home from work that day, she asked, "Why did I almost eat an entire box of crackers?" I knew in that moment I would get into trouble one way or another, so I lied and told her I didn't eat a lot of them.

Lady J was so infuriated with me over those crackers that she literally kicked me in the buttocks with her big yellow steel toe working boot. She kicked me so hard I remember stumbling into the bathroom which was connected to the kitchen and my room. I could feel the pain shooting throughout the area where I was kicked even when I tried sitting down on the bed. This wasn't the only time I would experience treatment of this kind. I wasn't the perfect child, but Lady J continued to be overbearing towards me for whatever reason. Sometimes part of my punishment would be that I couldn't attend church and what made matters worse is that it would conveniently be around the time we would have a program of some sort going on, and my participation was required. One time, a girlfriend of mine from church came by the house to see if I could attend church, but she was told no, I couldn't go. I don't know if Lady J truly realized how much going to church meant to me. I would be so sad and disappointed when I was denied being able to attend my "Safe Haven."

Not only did I have to deal with the punishment from Lady J, but I remember being disciplined by her companion. How he punished me for whatever I did wrong because to tell you the truth, I honestly don't remember what I did, but I do remember how awkward and uncomfortable I felt. He was an older guy who had an old-school way of disciplining children. I was a young, tall, and skinny girl; I was actually a little taller than he was when he told me that he was gonna to have to whip my behind. I was told to pull down my pants and lay across his lap so that he could spank me. I did what he said, and he whacked me a few times on my buttocks. I'll never forget how humiliated I felt. Maybe it was the idea of a man putting his hands on me, as he was the first man that whipped me instead of a woman. Or perhaps it was the flashback I'd had of the man and his son that had molested me when I was younger. As much as I dislike re-visiting those moments, they are realities that did take place.

I understand that back in those days, the way some parents dealt with children was completely different from how we as parents do things today. Yes, children are to be held accountable and disciplined according to how they behave and should be able to learn their lessons as they are being disciplined. The thing is, even correction and discipline should be done with patience, love, and understanding. I had no problem with being disciplined. I had a problem with "how" I was being disciplined. I'd already had quite a few traumatic experiences before I came to live with Lady J, and how I was placed with her added on to that pain. I felt there should have been more empathy and that some things should have been handled in a different manner. I was in a foster home for the first time in my life, living with someone I never knew existed on top of what had already transpired in my life before I moved there. I was hurt and couldn't see a way out of all the sadness and pain I'd harbored in my heart. The only time I felt safe and loved was when I was at church. So, you see, this is why I wouldn't tell D.C.F.S anything negative and made it appear as if everything was fine. I was too afraid to tell them the truth because by this time my church had become my lifeline. I told them what they wanted to hear in order to keep me where I wanted to stay, at least for the time being.

Needless to say, I felt lonely, but thankfully a few of the ladies at my church took me under their wings. I will refer to one of the women as Lady C. I'm calling her this because she was a woman who had so much compassion for the kids at church. She did not play when it came to us either! She wouldn't allow anyone to speak anything negative about us; she always came to our defense. Lady C holds an incredibly special place in my heart. She was one of the first ladies who pulled me into the choir when I joined the church. I remember her smile; it was so genuine. Her eyes were always full of love, and she didn't play with us kids either, but her being tough revealed her strength and protective nature towards us. Lady C always had activities and events for us to attend. All the long choir rehearsals, usher board practices, and sending us to sing all over the city paid off!!! Lol

Lady C always had a listening ear and would give me wise counsel. However, there was only so much she could do to protect me. I'm not sure if she realizes how much of God I saw in her because she allowed Him to use her to comfort me and so many others. She was one of the vessels God had chosen to pave the way for where I am now. My love for her runs very deep, and I will forever be grateful for her sacrifices. We would have those "on the ride home" talks, and when we would arrive at my house, she would sit with me in the car until I was "ok" to go in. I love that she took time out of her life for me. These are the things most people no longer take time for these days. Lady C had children of her own, and they didn't resent the attention I received from her, nor did they feel neglected by the attention that I received because they also played a huge role in my life. There is still a deep love that we have for each other to this day.

Another lady, who I will refer to as Lady D, also took time out of her life for me. Lady J would allow me to spend some nights with her. Lady C and Lady D were good friends. To me, they were like two peas in a pod. Lady D, may she rest in heaven, was like my saving grace. She had this infectious joy that would soften hearts around her. She had a soft spot for the kids in the choir. I think that's why the two ladies got along so well. I would spend a lot of weekends at her house since her daughter and I sang in the choir together, she and I became really good friends. We spent so many nights talking and cracking up with laughter until the wee hours of the morning. We would be so tired from being up all night, but we still had to be up and ready for church. We had to leave the house at seven in the morning to get to church for the eight o'clock service. Lady D's compassion was undeniable to all she came in contact with but make no mistake, she didn't play either! Lol, She and Lady C were very much alike when it came to us kids. I felt God showed special favor upon me because of how they treated me.

This was the "Safe Haven" I needed; that hedge of protection that I read about in the scriptures. The place where it was said, "…He will be with thee, He will not fail thee, neither forsake thee: fear not, neither be dismayed." Deuteronomy 31:8 It was my ark of safety, and although I didn't realize it, God was shielding me!

I loved my church family, and I enjoyed seeing their families come together in unity. I even enjoyed experiencing the love they showed me, but it didn't take away from the fact that I didn't have it shown by my own family during this time. There were many times I cried out to God for my mother. I loved my church, and the people there were my family, but there was still that missing piece in my heart. At times I couldn't help but feel as if I was borrowing love from other families that didn't belong to me. However, I was able to understand more about God's saving grace.

It had been a few years since I heard from my mother. All I know is I would talk to God almost every night about her. My faith in God developed to the level that I knew He could save my mother from the lifestyle she was living. I didn't know exactly what she was going through or what I was praying that God would save her from at that time, but I prayed and believed. I was now thirteen or fourteen years of age, standing in the gap for her in prayer. Now, this may sound strange; although I believed God could do what I prayed; I didn't fully understand that my prayers for her were actually reaching God's ears.

Throughout the years, my two elder sisters would call me now and again; by then, I had lost touch with my third sister, who lived with her father. We'd be so excited to hear from one another. Talking with my two sisters would always be hard for me because I missed them terribly, but we each had a bond that was never broken. I would always ask one of them to pick me up. Both of my sisters were about eight and nine years older than I was at the time; they were in their early twenties, living their own lives. Neither one of them was in a good position to care for me, and because I didn't mention anything I was going through, I believe they thought that I was better off living with Lady J than with them. Life for them hadn't been peaches and cream either. They lived their lives in pain, and sometimes pain causes one to make unwise choices. Those choices could have affected me had I lived with them, but I figure, hey, at least I got to speak with them.

We would talk for a while, and when it came time for us to end the call, I would try to silence my tears and hide the pain in my voice from having to say 'goodbye.' The love I felt from them through the phone at times was comforting but almost unbearable because I never knew when I would hear from them again. It seemed like every time I got a taste of their love, it could never stay with me, not even in the physical, only in my heart. My father had a family outside of me, and I couldn't see my mother and sisters. I felt such a void in my heart. During this time, I really latched on to God through His word, with the help of Lady B. It was something about her that I was drawn to. I honestly believe God sent her into my life! If I could describe her, I would say that she was like Deborah in the bible.

Lady B had so much strength, power, and bravery. Lady B had a way of pulling out of you what you had no idea was in you! What you could not see, she could see clearly. If you didn't understand how to express yourself or how you felt, she could articulate those feelings in such a way; you would have thought she was in your head. Lady B almost always had a strong and accurate judgment of character. If you thought you could get away with anything, you would be in for a surprise! She was not one you could not get over on. Lady B wouldn't beat around the bush; she would come at you in a straightforward manner, but she was gentle enough to help you understand your thought process if it was negative. Although I felt I took up much of Lady B's time, she made it clear that she was there for me. I was amazed at how she gave of herself unselfishly!

One Sunday afternoon, as Lady B and I were straightening the Sunday School classroom, she began to ask me questions, ones I had never thought of or considered. She and I had to have talked for at least four hours that day. She asked me questions like, "Where does God fit into your thoughts? Why do you think God allows certain things to happen to you in life?" I would express to her how I felt or what I thought, and she would come back with a different perspective and how I should look at things. It was then that I began to see God in a different light. He was not this distant God that just existed; He is the True God that's closer to me than I thought. I knew God existed in my fourteen-year-old mind because I heard about Him every week. I knew He heard our prayers, but I didn't know He answered them based on His timing. I knew God had a will and a plan for my life, but I did not connect that His Will was and is His Word.

The dots were being connected, and this was the beginning of my understanding of God regarding some things. I had to learn how to build a relationship with Him. I learned that whatever I asked should be according to His Will and not just what I desired. This was a new way of thinking for me, and it took me years to understand this. Lady B stayed on my toes so hard and did not pull any punches with me, but she encouraged me through it all. She was the Sunday School teacher at my "Safe Haven." Lady B encouraged us to think about whatever question she asked whether regarding a bible verse or a story she shared with us. She required that we apply God's word and what we learned to our lives. She took time to break down the verses in a way we could understand because she was big on making sure you were able to comprehend what you learned. Lady B would do this with us individually and outside of Sunday School. So many teenagers like myself were experiencing a tough time, and Lady B was there.

Lady B was dedicated! When I tell you, I had a one-track mind; it was pretty warped. Lol, All I can do is laugh when I think back to those times. Not that it's funny, I'm just amazed at how I can now speak on the condition of my mind during that time. I was young, but I was completely overwhelmed with what was going on back home with Lady J. Not to mention, it was still my desire to be with my mother, and even then, I was torn because I didn't want to be separated from my church home. I felt overcome by life in general. My mind literally felt like an overloaded flash drive. I couldn't see how I could view my life in a positive light or release what was harboring in my mind out so that it wouldn't take up so much mental space. I believe during this time, I was closed-minded about how I should have looked at my situation, but Lady B would help me redirect my thoughts and look at my life and those situations from a godly perspective. I truly needed the talk we had that day and all the other long and powerful discussions we'd have in the future. I truly thank God for ALL of the women He placed in my life (Lady C, Lady D, and Lady B)! They were and still are some strong and dedicated Sista's!!!

Chapter Eight

My Breaking Point

I always tried to hide what was taking place at home with Lady J, but as I got older, I'd gotten tired of the mistreatment and began to be a bit bolder in my stance with her. I always felt it would be better to be with someone in my daddy's family rather than be in my situation, but what could I do? I was now fifteen years old and at my breaking point. It would be the year I'd had enough of dealing with Lady J. I was at a crossroads. I had to decide on whether I should tell the truth to the D.C.F.S. or continue to stay in that hostile environment, all for the sake of staying at my Safe Haven. One of the things that the D.C.F.S. knew for sure was how strongly I felt about my church. I prayed that God would get me out of the situation with Lady J. Well, let me keep it real! I BEGGED God to get me out of there! It seemed as if the intensity and frustration between her and I was increasing each day. It's one thing to be disciplined but still be loved and cared for by an adult. It's a whole different ball game when you're being intimidated while being told to do something and not feeling loved.

Since I attended catholic school, it was mandatory that students wore uniforms every day. On the weekends, one of my duties at home was to iron all of the uniforms I would be wearing for the following week, so I wouldn't have to be concerned about it during the week, but there was a certain way I was told to iron them. If I didn't iron them to her liking,

I would have to keep ironing them repeatedly until it was done properly. During this time, Lady J wanted me to start answering her by saying, Yes or No ma'am, every time I needed to respond to her. Now, I'd already established just saying yes or no to her over the years. As a kid, I may have used the term "yeah" sometimes instead of saying yes, but it was an abrupt and unusual request to ask of me since she had never asked this of me before. Therefore, I couldn't understand why saying yes or no ma'am was being demanded of me at that moment. When Lady J told me to do this, I was not verbally taught to say, "yes or no ma'am," I was getting my behind whipped as I was being told to say, "yes or no, ma'am."

Well, Lady J wasn't pleased with how I'd answered her, and when I refused to respond to her the way she wanted me to, she reached over and hit me. I remember crying and backing away from her. We were in the kitchen, and there was no other room to enter; from there, the porch led to the back yard. So, Lady J continued to move towards me until there was nowhere else to go. I was up against a closed back door, and there was no room for me to turn around and open it. I was trapped while she was up close, in my face demanding that I say, "yes ma'am" to her. Every time I didn't respond, she'd hit me. It wasn't that I didn't want to say, "yes ma'am" to Lady J, nor was I intentionally trying to rebel against her. I was just tired of the mistreatment and controlling tone of her voice when I was already doing what I was told to do. For that reason, I refused to say yes, ma'am. I just continued to cry while taking the hits.

I know you're probably wondering why I didn't just say it, but from my experience during that time, I truly feel that if I said, "yes ma'am," it still wouldn't be the end of it. There would be another reason she would be displeased with, so I figured, what was the use of trying to please her? I felt it was impossible. Quite frankly, my brother or sister, I was tired of living this way, and I no longer wanted to be around anymore negativity; it was too much of a task trying to keep up with her demands. It's hurtful to think back on these memories, but in order to share my story, I must be transparent. Sadly, I believe Lady J disciplined me the only way she knew how but it was even more hurtful that I never heard I love you, not even once. Even if she did make an effort to tell me she loved me, I would have never believed her because her actions showed otherwise. So much had transpired living with Lady J along with everything else that happened over the years; it's only so much a person, even a child, can take.

One night, I got into trouble again, and Lady J called my father, who decided to come and discipline me. When he arrived, I managed to sneak out the front door, and I climbed into the backseat of his car. I thought he would eventually give up looking for me and go home; then, I would be at home with him and his family. I thought my plan would be a success! Welp!!! You can use your imagination, yup, that's right, I got busted!! They thought it was kind of funny, but for me, nothing was in the least bit funny! Things had gotten so bad I would take safety pins and make marks across my arms and wrist. Now, I wasn't suicidal; I began doing this out of desperation, just to get out of that environment! I guess with all the things that had already happened to me during my earlier years, my lashing out was becoming increasingly evident, and the day had come for me to take a stand against Lady J.

Lady J and I had this huge fight, and I felt like I was fighting for my life! To this day, I can't even tell you all of what the fight was all about, but I do remember defending myself verbally and her taking it as I was disrespecting her. I can still see the anger that was spewing out of Lady J, but this was the day that I was finally going to take a stand! It was also the day I thought I would lose my life! We both ended up on my bed; Lady J was on top of me with her hands around my neck. It didn't matter because I would no longer tolerate being a punching bag! We were wrestling, and of course, she was stronger than me, but somehow I managed to muster every ounce of strength (I don't know where the strength came from) within me, and I kicked her off of me. Lady J flew backward against the wall. Boy! Things popped off really bad after that happened. At that point, I was fed up, things had gone entirely too far! I don't know how the fight ended, but by then, I was at ***My Breaking Point,*** and my mind was made up! It was time to tell the Department of Children and Family Services the truth! It was time for them to place me into another home. I prayed to God that they would get me out of there, but please let me continue to attend my church every Sunday.

Please…

Chapter Nine

Music To My Ears

Soon after the incident with Lady J occurred, it was time to meet with the D.C.F.S. Usually, I would give them a good report by saying everything was going well with Lady J, and I would also speak very highly of my church home. Well, this was the day that I would spill the beans and tell the truth about everything that was going on. You would think that I'd be afraid and hold things back because I had no idea where I'd be placed, not this time! I told them the truth and expressed my love for my father's side of the family. I told them how I enjoyed being around them and wanted to be around them more often. They asked me the question I had been trying so hard to avoid; they asked, "Do you want to be moved from Lady J's home?" I took a deep breath and told them, "Yes, as long as I'm still able to attend my church."

A case with the D.C.F.S. was opened, and they began to do more investigating and questioning while looking for another placement for me. The caseworker I had been assigned to became very fond of me. It was like God sent her to me as my protector. She was very particular about whom I would be placed with, and she showed so much care and concern. This was another moment where I had to stop and think about the goodness of God! What I couldn't see back then, I most definitely see now. God's hand was always on my life; however, it wasn't without pain.

I had a break from school and was now at my father's house. Someone from the D.C.F.S. came by to speak with him. They wanted to know if he would permanently take me into his and mama's home. I remember walking in on the conversation just as the caseworker asked my father the question. His response was not only shocking, but it hurt me to the core. He said there wasn't enough room for me; they had three boys and his wife was the only one working at the time. I just stood there; I was devastated. I just couldn't believe that I was continuing in this cycle of not being wanted, even by my own father! That day it felt as if I had a giant hole in my chest! I went into one of my brothers' room, and the tears just started running down my cheeks. It felt as if my stomach was full of knots. One of my brothers saw me crying. I don't know how long it took me to get the words out so that he would understand what I was trying to convey to him. Bless his heart; he tried to comfort me as much as he knew how.

Arrangements were being made with the D.C.F.S. between my father, and Lady J. I would spend every weekend or every other weekend with his wife (Mama) and family. Later that evening, when my mama got home from work, I heard quarreling. I knew my brother had to have told her what my father said because you could hear her yelling at the top of her lungs. She was so upset with him, and I'm sure by then, he felt terrible. Although I never showed it, a wound remained in my heart for a really long time behind what he said. I thought that my daddy would have wanted to take me in after what had taken place between Lady J and I. Hearing the words, "there was no room for me," did something to my spirit; honestly, it broke my heart into pieces. Even then, I tried to justify his response by believing that maybe my dad didn't fully understand how horrible and serious life was and had been for me up until this point. It wasn't until years later that I was set free and able to give it all over to Jesus.

Although the D.C.F.S. was trying to place me in a home after speaking with my father, my grandmother(my father's mother) made it clear that she did not want me to be sent into the foster care system. My grandmother heard the news the same day and went to my daddy's house (she lived down the street from him) to try and calm my mama down, who was also upset with my daddy's decision. Through that situation, I could see the compassion she had for me. At that moment, my grandmother said something that would change the direction of my life. She said, "I would take you in if they would let me." I could not believe my ears! The idea of being around family was like ***music to my ears!*** I would finally be able to be around family members who, from my perspective, always seemed loving and happy to be in each other's company. I am sure this was just a pure delight to her as it was for me! My grandfather had recently passed away; they were together for many years; now, I would be living with her instead of living by herself. Of course, she had children that checked on her daily, but now she wouldn't have to be in the house alone. It was a blessing for both of us because now I would finally be surrounded by my own family, and it was a lot of them!

After reading my story until this point, I'm sure you can understand why this was so important to me. I was able to recognize why I needed this to happen for me at that moment. During that time, I was heartbroken and needed relief from the pain, abandonment, rejection, and constant abuse I was experiencing over and over again. So, to finally feel these good emotions welling up in my heart was something I did not take lightly. I felt we could now develop a real relationship as a family with this change! Oh, remember the one cousin I met that was the same age as me? We were now seeing one another again and could do lots of things together; we became best friends! I spent many nights over her house.

Even with the changes, I still wondered about my relationship with Lady J. I honestly don't remember having good times while living with her or having a good relationship. If there were any good days (and there were), they were from being able to spend so much time at my "Safe Haven." My focus in life while living with Lady J was more about getting through each day until I could survive on my own without being in the hands of those who were not able to understand that life was more than what they wanted for themselves. Even in this, I came to realize that God was and is always in the midst of every circumstance. Now I felt I had the chance to at least be happy.

Life was quite different with my dad's side of the family and what made things so interesting was everyone lived near each other. On one side of the street, my dad, his wife (Mama), and three brothers were in one household. My uncle, aunt, and about three or four of my cousins lived in the middle of the block. My grandparents lived down and across the street from them, and our cousins loved it! They all spent the night over their house. What could have been more exciting for me than living on 83rd street?! The same street that nearly your entire family lived on! Lol Anyone who ever hung out with my family would be considered a part of our family, which is why I stated that my family was the coolest people to be around. Everybody knew what was popping on 83rd! Lol

I've got so many memories of living on that street; good, bad, and ugly. I would need an entire chapter to tell those stories. I was learning a lot about myself, and as I grew older, I began to come out of my shell. I was also experiencing a whole new side to freedom in terms of speaking my mind, in a respectable way of course. It was all so new to me.

Chapter Ten

New Home

The time came that I would officially move in with my grandmother. I can only imagine what was going on in her mind. I'm pretty sure that the idea of her raising a teenager all over again had never crossed her mind, but it is my understanding that she was happy to have her granddaughter live with her! I can't even begin to express how grateful I am for her! I was almost sixteen years old when I was placed with my grandmother; it was just lovely; she had my room set up very nice for me when I moved in. I think the first night, my grandmother and I stayed up just talking. I know the Lord blessed my grandmother tremendously for taking me in! She had to move in a new home across the street from her old house and it worked out because then I was able to have my own room, the one she decorated. My grandmother had help from family, her church, and the D.C.F.S. Everything was provided for me so she would be stress-free! I know it was God who did this for her so that she could take care of me. He showed her special favor because He knew she would do her best to do right by me.

God answered my prayers in more ways than one! Not only was I out of the environment I was in, but I was still able to attend my church! One of the deacons who drove the church van would pick me up every Sunday morning. Wait, that's not all, my church wasn't only next door to my grandmother's church I was living with, but they were connected! I couldn't believe it! Sometimes I would attend afternoon services with grandmother and sing in their choir. I was now in church triple the time I would be at my own church. Lol. With that being said, let me stop right here and share something. There are many reasons why people assemble as the church, but I loved to fellowship with other like-minded Christians. I was not attending church because it was 'the thing to do' nor was I attending church just because it was my "Safe Haven."

Through attending my Safe Haven, I had come to learn some valuable tools in applying the Word of God to my life. I truly had some serious teachers of the Word of God that were called and anointed. I learned how to conduct myself as a Christian through the Word. We felt the Power and Presence of God, and you had no choice but to be convicted of whatever you did that was contrary to the Word of God, whether it was knowingly or unknowingly. We had godly mothers who made sure we understood the importance of walking upright before God, not just before the church members. The mothers used to encourage me so much, and I took everything to heart when it came to these things. Their words were effective because I saw them live what they taught.

God sent the people who "I NEEDED" to see me through those tough times to groom and shape me into the godly young lady I would become. He only allowed me to see the people who were doing right in the eyes of the Lord. So, if other things were going on in the church, God didn't allow me to see them at that time. I believe God shielded me from many things because He wanted me to stay focused on Him, His Word, and His love for me. After all, I already had a lot going on in my own life, and honestly, all I wanted to do was serve God. I know not everybody "does church" but we must understand that those in Christ are His church. (1 Corinthians 3:9 says, "For we are laborer's together with God: ye are God's husbandry, ye are God's building.") I am so thankful; God saved me from so much! I know I can never repay Him for what He's done for me! The least I can do is serve Him in the purpose and plan that He's chosen for me. This has always been my thought process; now, was I perfect? No! I failed God so many times! We all have different reasons as to how we started attending "church," every one of us has met God at different times in our lives, and where I met Him was literally in the church. I knew He was real and that he answered prayers!

I was now settled into a new home and was attending a new high school. I was finally around family, but I was constantly dealing with the D.C.F.S. They were now after my mother. I'm not sure if I've ever shared this with her. I would never tell them if I saw her because they wanted to turn her in to the authorities for some reason. It's not like I could tell them where she was anyway. When I did see her, I didn't know how I would find her, but somehow I always did. During those years, I learned how to catch the bus, and I would go and visit her from time to time. Life had really torn her down, but I continued to be in constant prayer for her. By then, I had developed a more mature relationship with God, and I now understood that He would answer my prayers regarding her....one day. The only thing that changed about my prayer is that I would no longer ask God for her to get me, but I would ask God to save and deliver her from every stronghold of drug addiction.

I'll never forget the day, I was sitting in my room as I did often, reading my bible, and I came across a scripture in the book of Romans chapter 10 verse 9, it said: "…If thou shalt confess with thy mouth the Lord Jesus, and shalt believe in thine heart that God hath raised Him from the dead, thou shalt be saved." My spirit leaped after reading that scripture. It was like a light bulb had come on in my mind, and I understood who Jesus was! Look, some of you may think I should have known that already; after all, I had been praying to Him to save my mother. You know, sometimes you think you got the gist of some things; sometimes it takes the Holy Spirit to help you to connect the dots of what salvation means until you finally get it! It was an 'A.H.A.' moment for me! It was also years later when I realized that God himself came through the womb of His own creation to be our Savior! That blew my mind for real! The more I learned, the more I grew spiritually.

Remember earlier in the chapters; I told you all about "the spot" my mother and her friends used to hang out at, where she also worked? Well, the club was just around the corner from where I was now living with my grandmother. I didn't understand then, but I was prompted to go to that club one day, and it just so happened that my mother was there. As I was walking, I saw her and called out to her. It looked as if she was high; her hair was not kept, she looked like she was in bad shape. I remember saying, "Mama, God loves you; if you just give your life over to Him, He Will save you." Remember this, my sister or brother; God said He would save my mother. What I did not know was that He would use me to speak those very words to her! Every time I saw my mother, I would tell her about Jesus. I didn't know how long it would be before seeing her again. My mother always tells the testimony that shortly after that day, she hit rock bottom, but God would answer my prayer and save her.

Chapter Eleven

Pent Up Emotions

I was now in high school, and I met some of the coolest girlfriends! We would stay over at each other's houses. I was the one always talking about God, and they would make fun of me. Lol, Hey, I figured after everything I'd been through, I couldn't help it because God was always my confidant, and it was pretty much the only thing I could relate to at that time. As far as I was concerned, God, church, and my life went hand in hand, but we were teenage girls who had many other things in common, and one of those things was daring one another to get into something we had no business getting into. As I mentioned before, I was now exposed to a different kind of freedom that I certainly didn't have before. Now don't get me wrong, my grandmother was strict but not controlling. I sure couldn't pull the wool over her eyes, nor could I get over on her, but I didn't get a whipping for every single thing I did wrong. Instead, she would tell me when she had a problem with something I did sternly, and later on, after she calmed down, she would hug and kiss me as if the incident had never happened.

Although she didn't have to, my grandmother verbally told me she loved me often. I knew she was telling me the truth because of her actions. I felt loved, and I was able to enjoy a somewhat "normal" life now. I was able to eat something out of the kitchen without asking for permission unless, of course, it belonged to someone else. I no longer had to worry about getting my behind kicked for eating crackers or if I ate them all because there was always plenty to eat. I felt a sense of relief because I was no longer with someone who always had built up frustration that caused a hostile atmosphere whenever they felt overwhelmed in their own lives. I no longer had to deal with anyone using me as their scapegoat in order to fulfill some sense of control through demanding I do whatever it was they wanted, no matter how harsh or humiliated it would make me feel.

I no longer had to worry about my pants being pulled down by someone I didn't know, all in the name of discipline. No, I didn't have my siblings surrounding me, but I had plenty of cousins who were like sisters to me and actually liked having me around them, although I talked about God ALL of the time. Lol. Based on what I knew about trying to live right and having a relationship with God, I always witnessed my family and friends. Now I didn't know that's what I was doing back then, but it would be years later that one of those friends would become an ordained minister of Jesus Christ! She loved telling others the story of how she made fun of me every time I talked to her and our friends about God, and now she is doing the same thing! Now she can't help telling others about Jesus! Hallelujah! As I think about this, I know my testimony was not in vain! I thank God for allowing me to be used by Him even when others thought I was crazy or knew me as what my friends called me, "the church girl"! Now each of those friends has a personal relationship with Jesus! Glory be to God!

It was just a blessing to be around others I loved, laughing, and sharing about what I was learning at "My Safe Haven." I saw and felt the genuine love my family had for me. It's something about being around family that makes you want to live and blossom every day! All of this felt new to me; having my family around was like having Christmas and Thanksgiving every day! Most of my family were so fun to be around; they were always full of laughter and love. We were very close to one another. On the other hand, there was a time in my life when I became this person that scared the living daylights out of me!

While in High School, I played basketball while going to church. I was focused on graduating with straight A's, but I made some choices during this season of my life that even took me by surprise! It was as if the pain and trauma of my past were controlling me. I began to feel the pain of rejection and abandonment that was buried deep in my heart since childhood. I don't believe I was consciously aware of those thoughts and feelings. I realized and later regretted participating in some of the things I thought were fun and acceptable to do because everybody else was doing them because they were NOT pleasing to God. I also realize that some of the unwise choices I made were only a cover-up to hide those feelings that had resurfaced.

One of those choices almost landed me in jail right before I turned eighteen. I got into an altercation with this young lady over a jacket, who I will refer to as Chloe. Yes, you read it right, but it wasn't just a jacket; it had a sentimental value. One of my aunts purchased the jacket, and another like it for my cousin and I. This was such a nice gesture and was one of the most expensive gifts given to me, and I wanted to cherish it. It was something of great value to me because there were many times I felt left out in some way or another, and in my mind, I thought this was my aunt's way of showing that she cared for me. Chloe was a young adult who was about 5 or 6 years older than me. Chloe and I did not have a close relationship; we were acquainted because of my family. Even if you weren't directly related, if my family developed a bond with you or your parents, they would automatically take you in as one of their own. The connection may have come through events or house parties they had which would be packed with people from the neighborhood, and if someone caused a problem with anyone among us, we would band together and defend each other if we had to. In other words, we had each other's back by association.

On the afternoon of my prom, some of my family came over to help prepare for my champagne party, which was a pre-prom party coordinated by my grandmother. We ate food and drank sparkling apple cider as a substitute for champagne. At this time, we were all in the kitchen. Some of my aunts prepared the food and set up decorations while my cousins just hung out. My cousin Fiona styled my hair. I loved it! She pulled half of my hair up into a bun but left some hair out in front to give me some bangs while leaving the hair in the back hanging. During this time, Chloe came over and found her way to the kitchen to chit-chat with my cousins and other family members. Then she randomly asked if she could borrow my jacket to wear for that evening. Without hesitation, I said, "No!" For some reason, it just didn't sit well with me that she even asked. I loved that jacket, and I didn't understand why she asked me if she could wear it for "my" festivities.

I guess my answer wasn't good enough, Chloe continued to ask me for my jacket, and I continued to tell her no. She then started pleading with me for it. Chole was not going to take no for an answer; I caved in and said yes but not without warning. I told her if anything happened to my jacket, "I was going to get her." After Fiona finished with my hair, I got my jacket from the closet and handed it to her, still warning her not to let anything happen to it. Everything in my mind was screaming not to let her hold it, but I gave it to her anyway and continued to get ready. A little later, I left to go to my prom, and when I returned home, I changed clothes because I was going to leave back out. A lot of my family was still at the house, and thinking back on it, I noticed they were kind of quiet. Something had transpired while I was gone, but they were trying to be cool about the situation and allow me to enjoy my day so, they didn't mention to me what happened.

It wasn't until a couple of days after my prom that my grandmother broke the news to me that Chloe had gotten into an altercation with someone, and my jacket was caught up against a fence and got ripped. I was so upset! I just knew something wasn't right when I came home! I immediately called Chloe and told her I was aware of the fight and that my jacket was torn. I told her she needed to get my jacket fixed, and I wanted it back soon. Well, I didn't hear from Chloe for about a week or so. It was now around the time of my graduation, and later that day, I came home to get ready for grad night, which was a popular high school event. All the graduating seniors would meet up and go to a place called Magic Mountain.

While I was in the bathroom getting ready, Chloe came in and handed me my jacket. She told me she took it to the cleaners for repair. The jacket's material was suede, and it was a rusty cinnamon, golden brown color. I took it from her but not without examining it. Immediately I saw that she had stitched it herself, and with light-yellow thread on top of that, it definitely wasn't done by a professional. It looked as if it had been sewn by a three-year-old. Needless to say, I was not happy! Chloe and I got into an argument because I wanted her to pay me for the damage that was done to the jacket, but she refused. To make matters worse, her attitude was horrible; she never seemed genuinely apologetic for damaging something so valuable to me. A couple of weeks after the incident, a few friends, cousins, my brother, and even Chole and I were hanging out on the weekend. We decided to walk to a store around the corner from our house to get beverages and snacks. Everyone was at the counter, ready to pay for their purchase, when an argument between Chloe and I broke out over my jacket. Chloe had been under the influence of alcohol, which caused her to be bolder in her stance with me. Eventually, we all left the store and returned around the corner to hang out between my parents' front porch and my aunt's front yard. Chloe and I were separated so we could both calm down; she went down the street and stood out in front of my parents' house while I stayed across the street in front of my aunt's house.

About 15 to 20 minutes later, I saw Chloe and some of my cousins walking towards me. I'm sure I had that "don't even say anything to me" look on my face as she was passing by. Just then, Chole became very hostile towards me, and she proceeded to jump in my face. Before I knew it, we were fighting! I don't know where the strength came from, but I picked her up and body-slammed her onto the concrete. My aunt overheard the ruckus and ran out of the house to break up the fight. She was yelling for me to stop. My aunt began to push and drag me to my house, which was a couple of doors down from where we were. The fight was so intense that my aunt pulled my shirt over my face so I couldn't see my surroundings in order to stop me from swinging on Chole. My aunt succeeded in getting me to the house; she pushed me in the door and told me to stay in and not come out.

I was in the house alone, and my hands were shaking, but as I sat there, I calmed down and snapped out of the rage I felt on the inside. I stood up and went to a mirror my grandmother had on the wall. I looked disheveled as I was trying to control my breathing. As I further examined myself in the mirror, I saw blood on my shirt and wondered where it came from. I started checking myself for cuts or bruises but didn't see any. I thought to myself; my grandmother is going to be so mad at me. Sure enough, a few minutes later, my grandmother stormed into the house, and she was hotter than fish grease! She began to go off on me, letting me know that the ambulance was there to take Chloe to the hospital and that she was going with her to make sure that she was all right.

I was so confused and dazed that I really didn't remember what happened, nor did I realize the severity of my actions and what I had done. I went to my room and tried to make sense of what was happening, but then my brother and cousin came into my room. Both of them were upset that I fought Chole, and they began arguing with me. It got to the point that I had to stand on my bed to wave them off of me. All I know is we started fighting. I mean, we fought from the back of my room to the front door, and we eventually ended up in the middle of the street; it was such a big mess! Never in my life had I been in a fight of this magnitude. It was by far the longest and most draining fight I had ever been in! Talk about drama!!! If I had a dollar for everything that happened on 83rd street, I would be a very rich woman right about now!

The police were called, and they wanted to question me, but because I was still a minor, my grandmother, Pastor, and other family members spoke on my behalf. My Pastor at the time offered to take me out to him and his wife's home until things calmed down. I agreed, as did my grandmother. When I arrived at their home, it was extremely late, but his wife was up waiting for me. She and I talked for a long while; she was so loving and kind towards me. She prayed with me, and before going to bed, I repented and asked God to forgive me. The following day, I woke up feeling very sore and stiff. I had such a hard time getting up, but I managed. Things died down, but I came to find out that Chloe had pressed charges against me. My cousin Fiona took me to court to face the judge, and he asked me to tell my side of the story. Chloe didn't show up; therefore, the case was dismissed! My sister or brother, let me tell you, this was a moment I saw God's grace in a way I had never seen before!

After everything transpired, all I could remember was how I prayed and even begged God to forgive me! It didn't matter if I was defending myself; I wasn't going to justify my actions; I had to repent. I came to understand that even if what happens is beyond you, you run the risk of making a bad decision that could impact your life if you don't take control of your thoughts. If the spirit of God does not lead you, you will find yourself walking in the flesh, and Satan will be there waiting to catch you off guard to lead you further down a path of destruction. The Lord worked in my favor, and the charges were dropped against me!

I took time to reflect on what happened that night to get to the root of why it happened. I had to admit that I wasn't just fighting Chloe. You have been on this journey with me, and I am sure you may know what I meant when I wrote that. I had a lot of anger and unresolved issues beyond Chloe and that jacket. There was no way I would have had that much strength and courage to fight Chloe had I not had all of that malice on the inside of me. After our fight, she had to be transported to the hospital. I believe what I endured in my childhood created many strongholds and bondages that caused my anger. I wasn't only fighting Chole but everyone who had harmed me. I don't believe that I would have fought her had I been set free from those feelings that seemed to have held me captive.

I knew that I wasn't displaying the true love of God behaving the way I did. I was still angry at my mother for abandoning me, but I couldn't take my anger out on her as she was nowhere to be found. I was too small, too young, and too innocent to fight with my molesters, one of which was over three hundred pounds on my six-year-old frame. I wasn't bold or old enough to stand up to Lady J because you are supposed to do what adults tell you to do. I was also too naïve to know there was a better way to parent or discipline a child, but at the same time, I was too afraid to leave because I believed I would be taken from the only place I felt secure in, and that was my "Safe Haven ."No matter how many times I spoke with others concerning my past, I still hadn't surrendered those feelings to God. In the process, I was fighting with all the anger I had bottled up on the inside of me. Although the jacket was sentimental, when I told Chloe that I would get her if she messed up my jacket, I didn't wake up that morning thinking that I would "literally" do it. As a result of her actions, Chloe was now included with those I felt had mistreated me in some way. She was a scapegoat for me to unleash my fury and pain, and that was the part that scared the living daylights out of me! I did not want to become the person I was becoming. However, I didn't come to understand all of this until adulthood, and that is when I truly surrendered my deep-rooted issues to God.

Despite all I endured, I finally graduated from high school and with honors! The D.C.F.S. also held a ceremony for graduates and selected designated speakers. I was among those who were chosen to speak. The ceremony was shown on new channels seven and four. I happened to be the first recipient to walk down the aisle. It was a moment of excitement for me! I received a full scholarship from the D.C.F.S. and my church! It was a great sense of accomplishment for me, but I know that it was God that helped me get to that place! This was the beginning of me becoming my own woman and no longer needing anyone to watch over me. It was time to move on to the next chapter but life as I knew it was about to get really real.

Chapter Twelve

Adulthood

I was now on my own; I got accepted into college and was able to stay on campus. My roommates and I became close, along with some other college buddies I met along the way; to this day, we remain good friends. It felt good to be independent; I was free to go places and do whatever I wanted without anyone looking over my shoulders. I was going to school while trying to maintain my post at church, praise dancing, and singing with the choir. By this time, I joined the young adult choir, and let me tell you, my brother or sister, if there was a time I needed to be a part of that choir, it was right then! Every song we sang hit me like a ton of bricks! Choir rehearsal wasn't just choir rehearsal, although we are the church; understand me when I say we didn't just practice, WE HAD CHURCH! The power and presence of God was felt every time we came together and sang! Needless to say, I was sad when I missed church; I was juggling school, work, and a few other things, but I was adjusting as an adult, it was a little challenging, but at the same time, it was liberating!

As I approached the end of my first year of college, I was asked to give a word of encouragement to the future graduates of the D.F.C.S. who were going to college. I was honored because I genuinely enjoyed encouraging others while letting them know if I could overcome the obstacles I faced in life and still make it to college, then they could too! As I mentioned, the ceremony made the news, the students were so encouraged, and I loved seeing the excitement on their faces as they moved towards their new life. Summer break was soon approaching, so I would have to move out of the apartment on campus. This also meant that I needed to decide where I would stay for the next three months until I could return for the following school year because my scholarship didn't cover summer semesters. I asked Ms. Olivia (my mother's cousin) if I could stay with her while I worked during the summer, and she gladly opened her doors to me. If you're wondering why I called my mother's cousin Ms. Olivia, as far as I know, there is no special reason; it's just what we all became accustomed to calling her. You may also wonder why I didn't go back to my grandmother's house for the summer break. Well, I contemplated moving back with her but changed my mind when one of my aunts made a statement that offended me a month before moving off-campus. It wasn't unusual for my aunt, who I will call Lola, to be blunt when it came to expressing how she felt. Before I share anymore, I want you to know that Aunt Lola was also one who shared some good nuggets with me over the years. She taught me how to be humble and respectful towards others. It's not that I didn't know or wasn't doing some of the things she shared with me already, but it was learning to be consistent in doing these things and not just when I felt like it. I never forgot those nuggets of knowledge she gave to me; I was and am incredibly grateful. However, this day as we were standing on Aunt Lola's sister's porch, she chose to address her feelings towards me aggressively. She complained that I had been slacking off when it came to visiting my grandmother. I mean, she had a mouthful of things to say, but out of everything said, it was one statement that stuck out to me like a sore thumb, and that was she felt "I was a burden to my grandmother," and "would be the cause of her going blind." I stood there burning with irritation, and as you could imagine, I was deeply hurt! I tried so hard to keep the tears from falling down my face. I couldn't believe she was saying this to me! I loved my grandmother, but I never tried to defend myself. There was no need to say, "Hey! auntie, that is not true!" At that moment, she said what she said and meant it; therefore, her mind was made up, but you know what the crazy thing was? I actually believed her and was fearful that something would happen to my grandmother if I stayed with her.

I truly felt my Aunt Lola's choice of words was harsh and that I was being misjudged. I was even more confused as to why she felt I might be the reason my grandmother could possibly go blind. Her words could not be taken back, and as much as I didn't want to believe what she said, I allowed those words to affect me deeply. I felt as if I was an outsider, and this actually caused me to stay away from my grandmother for a while. Besides the fact that I wanted to continue being on my own, I thought it was best for her and my sanity. I didn't want to worry or be afraid of something happening to my grandmother if I moved back in with her. So, for that reason, I decided to ask Ms. Olivia. After I got settled in, I still visited my grandmother and what she said puzzled me, only because of what my Aunt Lola said. My grandmother expressed that her feelings were hurt that I had not moved back in with her. She was so upset that she asked for her key back, so I honored her wishes and gave them to her through my cousin Renee. Here I was again, totally confused! Because of how my aunt spoke to me that day on top of what she said, I thought maybe my grandmother might have felt the same way. I realize now that I should have communicated to her why I chose not to stay with her. This truly hurt me, it took a while for me to get over all that happened, and honestly speaking, my heart was a little hardened towards my aunt and grandmother. Taking that key back did something to my spirit; for a moment, I felt out of place, and it was as if I didn't belong again. Now, you may have noticed that I didn't try to defend myself verbally. Well, it was my family's culture to discuss things among themselves before they did with the individual who was involved. Rather than sit down and ask the person how they felt about the situation, they would form an opinion about what they believed the person felt. The only thing that helped me stay positive was knowing what was in my heart. I would never try to hurt my grandmother or anyone else's feelings. Thank God my grandmother, and I were able to move past what happened that day, but I never told my aunt how what she said that day greatly affected my self-esteem, but she did apologize to me. We were standing on the porch outside my grandmother's door when she began to explain her motives for saying some things. I was incredibly surprised that she humbled herself and admitted that some things she said to me were offensive. Although she didn't say she was apologizing to me for that day specifically, I was still grateful. She was now practicing what she preached to me many years ago.

Summer break was over, and I returned to school. I was now in the middle of my second year of college. One afternoon while sitting in my dorm room preparing to write a paper for my English class, I noticed I had a missed call from my mother. She had gotten my number from Ms. Olivia, her cousin that I stayed with during my summer break. I didn't know her whereabouts; we hadn't spoken to one another in a few years, and this was the first time she had reached out to me. I sat on my bed listening to her voice message. I could hear the breaking in her voice as if she were about to cry as she was letting me know how proud she was of me and that she loved me. She also left me a contact number to return her call. Instead of feeling joy and relief from hearing her voice and knowing she was ok, I felt anger, rejection, and the pain I had suppressed all those years rising up again. I tried so hard to block those feelings from my mind as I called the number she left on the voice mail. Whenever I would see or speak to my mother, she always expressed how sorry she was for how things turned out with me, but I was tired of hearing it by this time. It was the same ole story. Sorry couldn't erase all that happened to me; we couldn't redo all the years stolen from me! She mentioned that she moved out of state and started a new life. That triggered something in me; well, that took me back to my childhood. From there, our conversation went downhill, and I noticed that she was now in defense mode. I remember thinking to myself, here we go again with the same song. Man! I really didn't want to hear the same story again! I had been through a lot myself, and honestly, I wasn't in the right frame of mind to understand what she was trying to convey to me. We ended the conversation with her being frustrated and hanging up the phone hastily, but she called right back to apologize. By that time, I was annoyed and felt more disappointment and resentment in my heart towards her than before.

After speaking with my mother, I'd always have moments where it felt as if I was reliving my childhood. I would go back to the nights when I would be up while everyone was asleep. I would be in my bed, under the covers holding my pillow tight, trying hard to muffle the noise by putting my fist in my mouth so no one would hear those deep-down ugly cries that came from the depths of my soul. I would huff, puff, and take deep breaths as flashbacks of every horrific scene replayed in my mind. Eventually, I would rock myself back and forth, hoping the pain resulting from everything that was done to me would go away. I wouldn't remember how long I'd be crying throughout the night, but I would wake up to a pillowcase soaked in my tears. You see, my brother or sister, my mother did not fully understand the extent of my pain, and those I did share some of what I went through only know a fraction of my story. Telling a fraction of my story was easier to express since I didn't have the courage or boldness to verbalize those deep secrets out loud. I didn't have the strength to speak out about what the molestations and abuse had done to my mind, body, and spirit. So, every time those thoughts resurfaced, I would mentally bury those memories and just not deal with them for a while.

I still had to function and move through everyday life. I was still trying to balance going to church and my studies, but I hung out with my cousin Renee during my free time. I didn't have my transportation during this time, but she did. Sometimes, I would take the bus from school to her house, or she'd pick me up. We spent a lot of weekends going to parties, to the mall, hanging out with friends, taking drives, or spending time on 83rd street with our other family members. We would have so much fun! Staying busy kept me distracted from the memories of my past. We were not yet twenty-one, but we got into some adult clubs by using our older cousin's I.D. cards to get in. Lol, Let me tell you, one of the things I hated doing more than anything was looking over my shoulders to see if someone was watching me. I would always be concerned that someone in the club would catch on to us, but hey, once we got in, I would have so much fun dancing and competing with others who thought they could dance better than me! If dancing was involved, I was there; it was one of my outlets. I didn't look at it this way at first, but dancing was my way of releasing stress and anxiety; although it may sound strange, it helped me escape feelings of loneliness. I enjoyed not having to think about what happened to me, but in the midst of the fun I was having, I didn't realize that I was in a backslidden state. Realistically, God was watching me, and it's not that I wasn't thinking of God; it's just that I wanted to do whatever kept the thoughts away, even at the expense of my spiritual walk. I thought I was just having fun because it was the thing to do. Honestly, I was doing what I wanted to do and having fun doing it.

I found myself getting frustrated towards the end of my second year in college because the scholarship that was awarded to me from the D.C.F.S. was not forthcoming in a timely manner. As a result of this, I began to apply for credit cards and get loans to help pay for my schooling. I could only do this for so long; it just made sense to find a job. Thankfully, one of my roommates put in a good word with someone she knew that worked as an attorney; he needed someone to work as his paralegal assistant. The job would consist of helping with cases related to bankruptcies, wills, and wage attachments. The most important part of my job would be delivering documents containing sensitive information. It was an important job, and I was grateful, but my monthly income was barely enough to cover the rent. I don't know what I would have done if it wasn't for the other scholarship funds I was receiving from my church to pay for other expenses such as my books and other necessities. I thought this would be the answer to my problem for a while, but unfortunately, the attorney had to shut down his business. But, while working for him I did come to realize that I was juggling too many things at once. Holding down a job and going to school took a toll on me physically and mentally; not only was I overwhelmed and feeling burnt out, but I also realized that I no longer wanted to do social work. Although I wanted to help children in foster homes by giving them hope and something to look forward to when they grew up, I realized that I would be too emotionally attached if something terrible happened to them. I just wouldn't be in the best frame of mind to do my job well. So, I changed my major to computer administrative systems. All the plans and goals I had set for myself came crashing down by then. I became indecisive about what I wanted to do, so I called Lady B, hoping she could help me sort out my thoughts because I no longer knew what I wanted to do; I couldn't focus while working and going to school. I had to repeat a few classes due to falling behind, and ultimately I had to take a leave of absence. I was so frustrated because I was determined to finish school! I wanted to be the first in my family to graduate from college and accomplish the goals that I had established in my life. Instead, I was too worried about having to pay for school. I couldn't even use the rest of the funds from the D.C.F.S because they had to go towards the late payments owed to the apartment manager on campus. I reached out to Lady B, and thankfully, she invited me to stay with her until I could get back on my feet and return to the campus. Lady B wasn't home much; her job was out of town, so I would stay at her house and maintain it while she was away. This also afforded me the freedom to do some of the things I will share later.

Shortly after moving in with Lady B, I started working with a temp agency at a local hospital as a general office clerk in the medical records department. I did this during the day, and in the evenings, I worked a second job at a local restaurant as a cashier and greeter. I was still in contact with my caseworker from the D.C.F.S, who told me about a program that was a great opportunity and thought that I would like this pace a little better than the traditional college setting for the time being. It was a travel academy school that required me to take an intense ten-week course, and afterward, the school would help me find a job as a travel agent paying a decent wage. I agreed with going through the program, and during the time the position at the hospital was ending, I got accepted into the travel academy school. I was also transferred to one of the nearest locations of the restaurant chains I was working with, so my commute between Lady B's home and the school would be much easier. The school's location was about 45 minutes away from where she lived, so I would leave the house early enough to make the class which lasted from 8 am until about 4 pm. When the class ended, I would change into my work uniform and then head to my job at the restaurant. It took me about 20 to 45 minutes to get there depending on the traffic, and sometimes I barely had enough time to start my shift which began at 5:00 pm and would end between 10 pm and midnight if I worked overtime. This is where I met and became friends with a coworker who I will refer to as Vivian. She was an older lady with a young heart and personality. We maintained a friendship outside of work that lasted for a couple of years. The first day we met, we bonded like we had been buddies for a long time. There were times she treated me as a sister, but there were also times where it felt as if she was being "motherly." Vivian introduced me to her brothers, who would come and pick her up from work. One night they came to give her a ride as usual, but this time they invited me to join them for some fun because they were hosting a party. I accepted the invitation; after my shift ended, I went home to change my clothes, and then I headed to the party. When I arrived, Vivian introduced me to some of her other family members; everyone was cheerful and dancing. I joined in with the crowd and thought to myself, wow, this was cool! After the party was over, I hung out a bit longer before going home. After that night, Vivian and I started going to clubs pretty much every weekend. By now, I had a car, so I would be the designated driver while she paid my way into the clubs. I was almost done with school, but Vivian lived closer to the travel school, so on the weekends, when we went out dancing, I would stay over at her place instead of driving back home. She had three teenage children, and sometimes we would all hang out, which was just about every weekend unless I had choir rehearsal on Friday nights, but I made sure I was back home by Sunday.

One night something interesting happened; Vivian and I went out to a club, as usual, to go dancing. I had considered myself the designated driver by this time and not just because Vivian didn't have a car. I no longer felt like I was hanging out with a friend but someone who was simply doing a chore. After sitting for a while watching my friend dancing and having a good time, I excused myself and went to the lady's room. Upon entering, I saw two ladies talking. When I finished using the restroom, they were still conversing. At this point, we were all facing the mirror. I overheard one of the ladies sharing what was happening in her life. Their conversation ended, and one of the ladies left the restroom. Now it was only her (the one sharing her issues) and I in the restroom. Normally I wouldn't engage in other people's conversation, I didn't know what came over me then, but now I know that it had to be the Holy Spirit that caused me to minister to this lady. I began to tell her that God loved her. She was in front of me facing the mirror, so we watched each other through the mirror as I spoke to her. I didn't know this lady before this day, but there I was ministering to her. I said some things to her that prompted her to ask me, "Who are you?" I told her that I was just a girl who loved God and that she needed to know that God loves her as well. I was speaking, but it was God speaking through me. I believe I had seen her at another club before, so it was as if it was a divine appointment for us both. She appeared to be much older than I was at that time. Here I was, talking about God in the midst of worldly things, yet God still used me to speak to that lady! By then, I was no longer enjoying the club we were in or the music playing. I just couldn't come back from what happened in that restroom. I was in a whole different mood after that. Vivian and I left that club, and at that point, all I could talk about was God. I never forgot about that night or how the Lord used me.

Let me pause right here, my brother or sister; I am not justifying my actions. I want to express something here; as I stated earlier, I didn't realize that I was in a backslidden state, nor did I know that my reason for going out and keeping busy was to dismiss the pain and rejection I felt for years. I went from clubbing to drinking, and although I knew some of the things I was doing weren't right in God's sight, I didn't fully believe that I was wrong for doing some of those things. I felt that if I wasn't abusing alcohol, it wouldn't affect my relationship or walk with God, so I continued with this lifestyle until I was older. In my mind, I wasn't hurting anyone, and I was just having fun. I got in the clubs for free; I enjoyed dancing, and because I was always the designated driver, sometimes it helped me not to consume too much alcohol. Now there were times I did drink a little too much, and as a result, there were a few times that I got drunk but, I didn't do it regularly. These were all the things I would tell myself, and I figured, hey, you're not destroying your body. Most times, I would drink as a dare to do things I wouldn't normally do had I been sober. Later, I found myself in a compromising position with someone I was in a relationship with, and guess what, drinking gave me a boldness I didn't have while sober, and it allowed me to relax and give in to what my body (flesh) desired. Drinking became an escape and an excuse to cut loose! If I had a drink, I would turn into someone else on the dance floor, and I would dance more provocatively than I would have, all while knowing deep inside I had no business doing any of it. The fun I was having drowned out any feelings of conviction.

Did I have to have a drink? No. Even when I did drink, I was always conscious of God, always knowing that He knew my every thought and watched my every move. It wasn't until years later that I realized I couldn't do what I wanted or live any way I wanted to. I had to make the decision to live for God or let my flesh continue to rule over me. I was around Vivian and her family for less than a year, but I noticed significant changes. Needless to say, hanging out with her was beginning to get old, not only with driving her around everywhere she wanted to go, but her demeanor changed towards me. I was almost twenty years younger than her, and with her being a mother of three teenagers who were nearly adults, she was beginning to get a little bossy. The relationship looked more like a parent and child relationship than a friendship. A night out with Vivian confirmed it for me. She and I were leaving the club, and as we were approaching my car, I could see that some glass had shattered on the ground. When we got closer to my car, I noticed that someone had attempted to break into my vehicle. I had a white Nissan Sentra at the time; thankfully, I didn't have anything valuable inside, but they had stolen the hub caps off of my tires! I was shocked that they had chosen my car out of all the nicer ones. It wasn't Vivian's fault; of course, if anything, it was my fault for hanging out with her as much as I had; it just felt like it was always something crazy happening every time we were together. This incident made me question why I felt so drained every time I was around her. Something wasn't right, and I sensed that the Lord was telling me that I needed to slow down a little and figure out something else to do with my time so, I stayed home (Lady B's house) more often. I knew I needed to make some changes.

Not long after, I graduated from the travel academy and was waiting for a job to become available so I could begin working as a travel consultant. In the meantime, I was still working at the restaurant. I would take the Pasadena Freeway often for my commute to work. On this particular day, I was listening to the song "More than I can bear" by Kirk Franklin. I was driving on the far left of the freeway, it was bumper-to-bumper traffic, and it began to rain. As I listened to the words, my spirit felt uplifted! I was singing and praising the Lord when all of a sudden, my car began to slip and slide. I was almost in the opposite direction of the freeway! I wanted to panic, but something on the inside of me said **No**! I knew that I needed to take control of the car. I don't remember where I learned this, but it came to mind that you have to turn your steering wheel in the opposite direction to prevent the car from going on the opposite side of the road. Thank God I managed to do just that; I grabbed hold of the steering wheel and turned it sharply in the opposite direction, away from the other side of the freeway heading south. When I did that, my car spun around in the middle of the freeway!

My sister or brother, when my car spun around in the middle of that intersection, I could have sworn I had seen something white flashing above my head, like a silhouette going around in circular motion. I believe what I saw was the presence of Angels, and they were all around me! Mind you, I was in bumper-to-bumper traffic, but there was not one car in front of me and not one car behind me! I was the only car in the middle of the intersection! God gave me enough time to turn my car around the correct way and drive forward. By that time, all the cars came rushing behind me back into traffic, but there was still enough distance between me and those cars. By the time I entered back into the traffic, the perfect song had begun to play. It is called "So Good" by Kirk Franklin, and the lyrics say, "I could have been dead and gone, sleeping in my grave." Indeed, God has been so good!!! Let me tell you, my brother or sister; I began to praise God, yelling, "Thank you, Jesus!" for the rest of the 25 to 30 minutes it took to get to work! When I got to work, I told everyone who had an ear to hear, and every time I did, I would give God glory and praise again! Only not as loudly as I did in the car. Lol, I knew God had spared my life once again! I don't think I looked at it this way back then; it would be years later before I would even begin to have a clear understanding that this was a direct attack of the enemy! After the incident with my car spinning on the freeway, I started the job as a travel consultant a few weeks later. I was responsible for arranging domestic and international travel, calculating car fares, and making hotel reservations. It was about 13 minutes from Lady B's house, which was a way better commute. After working for a while, I started saving up to get my own place. Meanwhile, my mother and I were slowly trying to build a relationship. Now our conversations were not as offensive and were more tolerable. We would talk on the phone but not too long, just briefly, to say hello and check in with one another. One day at work, while I had a moment between calls, I started randomly searching for cheap flights to where my mother was now living. I happened to find a really good deal, and on top of that, I was able to take advantage of my employee discount. I booked a flight for that following weekend. I called my mother to let her know that I would be coming to visit her, and we made arrangements for her best friend, Fran, to drive her to pick me up from the airport. My sister and her husband were also going to drive 3 hours to meet up with us.

I hadn't seen my sister since I was about eight years old and maybe one time very briefly after that. I hadn't seen my mother since I was 15 or 16 years old. I was so excited about flying on an airplane to another state, and I was really looking forward to seeing my sister! As for my mother, I was more reserved. It's not that I wasn't happy to be visiting her; I just didn't know how to feel. I got off the airplane and went to baggage claim to retrieve my luggage, and that's when I saw Fran and my mother waiting for me. We were all excited to see one another! My mother, who is 6 feet tall, smiles from ear to ear and gives me this big ole gigantic hug! She literally smothered my 5 feet 7 inches against her tall frame; I had to laugh so that I could breathe. This was my first meeting with

Fran, but I had spoken with her a few times over the phone, we each greeted each other with a hug as well. Fran got into the driver's side, and I hopped into the back seat while she drove us back to my mother's place. My mother would look back every 2 minutes at me and smile just as I remembered her doing when I was a child. This was the first time in a long time I had seen her completely sober; she looked like she was in a better place in her life now that she had given her life to God. She sounded happier; she had good, honest, and loyal friends; it was as if she was a free woman! When we got to my mothers' apartment, she introduced me to the security guard and every neighbor we passed by; she said, "Hey, this is my beautiful daughter, isn't she pretty?!" After the first few times of being introduced, I was ready to get in and settle down. Lol My mother and I finally got settled into her place; it was already late, but we talked for a while. She briefly shared her past and how she didn't have a good childhood coming up, and she told me how several tragedies in her life led her to look for love in all the wrong places. She told me about the abusive relationships among her family and that she had been violated. My mother expressed how she didn't feel wanted or loved and had very low self-esteem. She expressed how she and my dad got together and how I came into the world. It was evident that my mother had gone through so much turmoil in her life. This helped me better understand why things had turned out the way they did, but it was still a lot to take in. There was so much more to her story, but she only shared the parts she felt comfortable with. For some reason, I felt that I still had something I was holding on to, but I couldn't pinpoint exactly what it was. Eventually, I dozed off to sleep; I don't know if she slept at all. I had this feeling that she was watching me all that night.

The next day we planned to meet up with my sister and her husband at Fran's house. Fran had a nice dinner, and while we were eating, my sister finally came in. We greeted each other with the longest hug! My sister ended up staying with my mother and I. We all laughed, joked, and reminisced. I can even remember praise dancing for them! Eventually, we went to sleep and got ready for church the next day. After service, we took pictures, and my sister and her husband announced that they were leaving. When my sister turned to say goodbye, I broke down and cried so hard while wrapping my arms tightly around her waist. It was one thing to talk with her over the phone, but another when getting that infectious love hug, especially from your sibling, who you know truly loves you! I could feel my heart kind of breaking again; it felt like I was seven or eight years old again, having to leave, not knowing when I would be able to see her again. We both held each other tightly until we had to let each other go. My sister and her husband had to get on the road and take that 3 to 4-hour trip home. Everyone was shedding tears that day. I felt sad, we had such a good time, and I really didn't want that feeling to end, but it was time for me to change clothes and prepare for my flight back home. It was kind of quiet on the ride to the airport, and when we arrived, I had to wait maybe a good 20 to 30 minutes before I was to board the plane. My mother sat to my left and Fran to my right; just then, my mother asked me, "How come you aren't crying for me like you did your sister?" I sensed that she felt that I loved my sister more than her because I didn't have the same reaction with her as I did with my sister. In my mind, my sister didn't hurt me the way my mother did. I really didn't expect her to ask me that, but I remember saying to her, "I've cried enough over you." Now, that may have sounded harsh, and it wasn't my intention to hurt her feelings, but that was what I felt at the time. My mother and sisters were in two different categories when it came to this situation. My mother never responded; she remained silent. What did surprise me the most was hearing Fran express her feelings towards me. She cried tears of joy and said she loves me and considers me like a daughter. She told me she was glad I had come out to visit them. She said a few other things, but that stood out to me. I didn't realize how affected she was by our visit. It was now time for me to board the plane. We all hugged each other, and I turned to hand my ticket over to the ticket agent. After I sat down and buckled up, that's when I felt the tears trickling down my cheeks. I sat there thinking of the events that took place the entire weekend, and I concluded that I was really tired of saying goodbye. I didn't know if I would ever enjoy having the whole family together in one state and for a longer period of time. It felt like the good times always got cut short. I sat in the chair and dozed off to sleep, feeling emotionally drained.

I continued working and finally came to a place where I was financially stable. I saved up enough money to get my first apartment, and Lady B blessed me with her entire living room set! I was so grateful for her generosity! She had enough patience to walk me through my process and gave me enough space to let me figure things out for myself. I've learned a lot from Lady B; she is a well-educated and classy woman of God. Everything about her radiates power and authority. She always exemplifies strength everywhere she goes! She is a businesswoman who handles things with such poise and professionalism. She set an example for me that I try to imitate even today. I'll never forget the lessons I learned from her, one of which I'll always remember. I was driving Lady B to a location, and she dropped a wisdom nugget using a lane on the freeway as an example. She said when you are driving on the freeway, one lane may be bumper-to-bumper traffic, and the other lane may be going at a faster pace. You may start in the lane that is bumper to bumper and decide to jump into the lane that is going at a faster pace, only to see that this lane is coming to a slower pace and the other lane that was bumper to bumper is now going at the speed you were hoping to go at. Sometimes we don't have the patience to wait; we feel like things are taking too long, and we want to hurry to get to our destination. Had we waited it out, instead of taking the route we felt was faster, we would be at our destination on time. Instead, we find that we are further back than we should be. There are also times when the Lord may nudge us to get into the faster lane, but we have gotten too comfortable with the pace we're going, and we find ourselves regretting that we didn't move when He told us to. This blessed me, and it made me realize how much I had to be sure to follow the leading of the Holy Spirit.

So, I was now settled in my first apartment and I felt like a grownup with all of the responsibility of having to pay my own bills. My commute to work was now about 25 minutes each way. My schedule was from 6 am until 2:30 pm, which gave me time to do anything else I needed to do that day. Vivian and I were communicating but not as much as we had before. Vivian contacted me within a week or two of moving into my place. She lost her apartment and needed to find another place for her and her children to live. Without a lot of hesitation, I opened my doors to her. It was supposed to be Vivian by herself while her children stayed with their father or other family members as they all were in close proximity to one another. Well, it didn't take long for things to go downhill. Vivian's and my schedule were opposite of one another. I worked all day Monday through Friday while she worked odd shifts, so we barely saw much of each other during the first couple of weeks. Her kids and nephew ranging between the ages of 15 to 18, would come over to the apartment. That was fine until they began spending the night. Then one night turned into multiple nights, and the problem with this was it wasn't in our agreement for her nephew and older kids to stay there, per her suggestion. On top of all of this, my car broke down. I had blown the head gasket off, and I couldn't afford to get it fixed right away, so I had to come up with another option to get to and from work. I ended up asking my old college roommate if I could stay with her since she lived about 6 minutes away from my job. She agreed and took me back and forth to work. I also made payment arrangements for my car to be fixed with my cousin Renee's boyfriend, who worked as a mechanic. I slept on my college roommate's sofa until I could drive again while Vivian stayed at my apartment.

While waiting to get my car fixed during those few weeks, I received a call from my apartment manager warning me that there were complaints of loud music being played late at night, disturbing the other tenants. I was told if I didn't keep the music down, I would be asked to move out. I called Vivian to ask what was going on, and she said the music wasn't as loud as the people claimed it to be. Knowing Vivian, I knew the music was loud, but she gave me her word that she wouldn't play it at the volume it was again. I was trying to be polite because Vivian had been nice enough to let me stay some nights with her. However, I felt that she was beginning to take advantage of my kindness. She also broke our agreement and let her nephew and children move in while I was gone, but the worst part is they had no respect or concern for me or the other tenants. About a week or two later, I got a call from Vivian stating that I had a notice on my apartment door and that it needed my attention right away. I managed to get a ride to my apartment to receive a notice from the manager giving me 30 days to move out. I called the apartment manager immediately and tried to see if there was anything I could do. Vivian wasn't supposed to be staying with me, so there was no way to defend myself, and I knew the manager at the apartment wasn't lying. I was told that music was being played all hours of the day and night. Again, Vivian was older but young at heart. She almost acted the same age as her children, so I knew she contributed to the loud noise. Needless to say, this caused tension between Vivian and I but what was most hurtful was that she had a nonchalant attitude about the situation, so I knew it was time to do something.

I had already paid the rent for the month, so I needed to come up with the security deposit for another apartment. We'd already established that Vivian needed to move out soon, but I thought to myself, why should I let her stay rent and utilities free when she is the one that caused me to get evicted out of my apartment? I needed to save all the money I could, so I told her that she needed to leave soon because I needed to find somewhere to live fast. I also had all the utilities cut off, and she still wouldn't leave the apartment.

My car was finally fixed and ready to be picked up, I found another apartment near my job, and now it was time for me to grab my clothes and a few other things I could take with me. Now, I'd only lived in the apartment for a couple of days before the fiasco took place! I drove to my apartment, and upon entering, I saw that Vivan had the gas and lights turned back on, but this time it was in her name. Vivian had cooked, and her children were there sitting around, just chilling and relaxing. The tension among us was so thick you could cut it with a knife! Vivian was trying to be cool at first, but I knew she was mad, and so was I. I proceeded to my room to pack my clothes, but first, I went into the kitchen to get a fork so that I could use it to poke a hole at the bottom of a large black trash bag to pull the hangers through the hole and slide the plastic over my clothes. As I was coming out of the kitchen, Vivian and I started exchanging words about why I turned off the electricity and who was wrong. Vivian did the unthinkable; she kicked me right in the middle of my stomach! I stumbled a couple of steps backward, but now, I was hotter than fish grease! I hadn't had any kids yet, and I didn't know if she had damaged anything; that's how hard she kicked me! I took a couple of steps back, then I ran towards her and did a Bruce Lee karate kick so hard against her mid-section until I saw her stumble backward and hit the wall. Just as we were getting ready to run toward each other again, Vivian's daughter decided that she wanted to make things a little more difficult by trying to jump in the middle of us. Somehow, Vivian, her daughter, and I were all wrestling with all of our hands up in the air! I still had the fork in my hand, and at this point, they were trying to remove it, but I held on to it. Vivian's son or nephew grabbed her daughter while the other jumped between me and Vivian. The nephew tried to get me to calm down by escorting me into the bathroom but by that time, I was livid!

I called my cousin Renee and asked her to come over to the apartment since I knew she'd have my back. After I got off the phone, I went to my room to finish packing my clothes. I was getting angrier the more I packed! I thought to myself, I never even had the chance to sleep in the room of my first apartment, and here I was having to leave while she was in my apartment cooking and relaxing! Renee arrived about 10 minutes later, holding a heavy iron steel pole. She stood by the door slapping the pole against her hand, looking like she was ready for battle while I transferred my clothes from my room to my car. By this time, everyone had settled down and was probably too tired to have another go around in the boxing ring! Myself included, although at the moment I felt like Rambo! Man, it took so much of my energy fighting and arguing with four people in one evening, and once my adrenaline had come down, I felt worn out! I moved out the majority of my things but decided that I would come back for the rest later. My thirty days were almost up, so my dad and I went to the apartment. Thankfully Vivian and her family were nowhere in sight. After that ordeal, I decided to be cautious of who I chose to be friends with. I was glad it was over, and I was now settled in my new apartment.

Chapter Thirteen

How I Overcame My Past

I was now officially in my new apartment, and this time I would live alone. I was still attending church, but it seemed as if life was becoming more of a struggle, and I was holding on by a thread. The majority of my paycheck went towards rent, electricity was high, and at times, I barely had enough money to put gas in the car or buy food to eat. I thought living on my own would help me get a better grip on life, but it seemed like nothing was going right for me. Come to think of it, I had yet to include God in any of the decisions I was making, and I'm talking about simple things such as asking the Lord, where do you want me to go? What do you need me to do next, or where do you want me to live? Instead, I was questioning myself and asking, "Where did I go wrong?" It was time to change the direction that I was going.

I found myself depending on God in a way I never had before; it was also all I knew to do, I believed He would provide, and He did just that. When I had no food in my refrigerator, God would make a way, and I would be able to eat. These were little miracles that would occur, and I would find joy in knowing that He cared about my needs. During this time of struggle, the emotions I tried to keep suppressed throughout the years began to resurface. One day, as I laid on my living room floor, I started talking to God about the issues I was having with my mother. The more I thought about the things that took place in my life, the more those feelings of resentment would come over me. I figured since those feelings kept coming up, it was ***finally time*** to confront them. It was not only time to pray for my mother but to have a serious conversation with God. I let it all out because I knew He was the only one who could deal with my anger and pain, but at that time, deep down inside, I was angry with Him.

Yes, I was angrier with the people who did those things to me, but I was confused as to why they were allowed to happen when He had the power to stop it. I threw out so many questions at Him. I yelled out that they could have caused me to go crazy, or I could have done to others what they had done to me! I hollered loudly, "They did not have any right to do what they did to me, so why God!? Why?!" I remember telling God that the pain hurt so bad! I told Him I wanted to forget everything that happened to me. I begged Him to take the memories away from me because they consumed my mind all of the time. In fact, I said to the Lord, "I don't want anyone near me, especially if I can't trust them!" I thought it would be easier to live by myself and be alone so no one could take advantage of me. I remember saying, "Lord, I still don't understand why this had to happen to me!

This is a lot to deal with God!! I'm hurting!! I'm angry!!! Can't you understand what I am going through here?" It was as if I had a wrestling match with God. I felt drained, and my eyes were swollen from so much crying; my head was swimming from being laid out on the floor for hours, just pouring out my heart, hurt, and frustration to God, but what happened next threw me for a loop. I remember hearing God's voice clearly. He asked, **"If you were to leave this earth today, if you were to stand before me and I ask you, daughter, why haven't** you done the things that were required of you? What would your answer be?" I began to think, what was I going to say? Was I going to blame my mother for not doing her part as a mother; therefore, justifying why I was doing "me"? That question provoked me to ask myself, "Why did I do the things that weren't pleasing to God?"

Just then, these very words fell in my spirit. **"Your mother will have to give me an account for what she has done, but you, my daughter, will also have to give an account for what you have done as well. You can no longer use your mother as an excuse for not doing what you are required to do in this life. You can no longer blame your mother for what she has done to you. You will be held accountable for your actions and the decisions you've made. You must forgive her just as I have forgiven you. You must forgive to be forgiven. (Matthew 6:15, KJV) My daughter, have you considered that your life could very well be used to help save your mother's life? I put in you the love you have for your mother and the desire for her to know me and be saved because she, too, has a purpose. Remember all those times that you prayed for your mother's salvation? Remember when you were young and how you shared your love to her for me? At the age of 15, you told her about me. You told her that I was the only one who could save her if she gave all her problems to me. It was my voice that spoke through you; I was the one who was drawing her to me as she was getting ready to take that last hit of drugs. She has to go through her own deliverance; I need you to understand that I love you with an everlasting love, and because you have shown your love for me by telling her about me, she is now building a relationship with me."**

Now I understood why I could not pinpoint what I was still holding on to when I went to visit my mother that weekend. I had not let go of the grudge I harbored towards her. I felt that what she went through in her past had nothing to do with me. What did I do wrong? I was just a child?! I didn't treat her like everyone else did; I was innocent in all of this! But ultimately, I realized that I had to finally let it ***All GO!!!***

All I could say to myself was, "My God!". At that moment, the Lord made it very clear what part of my purpose was; despite all of the pain I experienced, and I cried my heart out! I was by myself on the floor for what seemed to be hours. I was finally dealing with the feelings of abandonment, deep hurt, pain, rejection, resentment, wounds from the past, the abuse I suffered and had been carrying all of my life. I decided to confront those feelings and face them head-on while releasing them to God! I thought about all the things I had done because of what took place in my life as a child; the drinking, partying, and clubbing wasn't even what I truly desired to do. I was only masking the pain I felt. I realized that I had to repent and acknowledge my Lord as Savior. I was not only shedding tears, but it was as if I was also shedding weight from the bondages of molestation and the beatings that tried to break me down as a young girl. I received love from God that nobody in my life knew how to give during that time. I felt God's presence come in the room, and He wrapped **"His Loving Arms Around Me."** It reminds me of a song our young adult choir used to sing called **"Keep Your Loving Arms Around Me"** by Milton Brunson and The Thompson Community Choir.

Not everyone at my church knew all of what I endured as a child, and songs like this one was a reminder of God's love for me. That day I finally released everything and surrendered it all to God, and when I sang in the choir, it was as if more deliverances in my life would take place! It was like a revival for me every Sunday! Now don't get me wrong, what God did in me while I was on that floor was amazing and powerful, but I continued to walk out my deliverance. Over time, the Lord revealed the many different ways I was able to heal. Remember the women I mentioned from my church? Through them, the Lord showed me how deeply concerned He was for me. These women took time out of their lives for little ole me. He sent Lady D so that I would see His compassion in her eyes; through her, He wanted me to see how He never took His eyes off me. He wanted me to see how much He loved me and that there were still good people in the world.

The Lord also showed me His protection through Lady D, although it was for a short period of time. She would take me home from church, and it was during those times, I felt comforted. She made me feel at ease before going "home" to face Lady J. He sent Lady B to help me realize that I had more in me and could do more than what I believed I was capable of doing. With her, I realized that the Lord was closer than I imagined. God used her to show me what strength and courage looked like, so in the future, I would come to understand and know who I was in His Son Jesus Christ. Lady B provided me with wise counsel. I saw what it looked like to walk upright before God through her. She was His example for me, so I would know what a person's life looks like when they grow and mature in His Word.

The Lord sent Lady D to reveal His Joy. No matter what was going on in her life, His Joy would **shew (Shew means God's reveal; show is the world's reveal)** through her. It was indeed joy that the world did not or could not give nor take away from her. I learned the true meaning of joy looking at her life. I also learned that we could choose to give up our joy. The Lord sent those ladies to me and He gave them the grace, patience, and love I needed to guide me, to sit with me, to listen and hear my pain so that I was able to sort out my feelings and learn how to cope with all I was enduring. The Word of God says in Proverbs 19:20KJV, "Hear counsel, and receive instruction, that thou mayest be wise in thy latter end." My brother or sister, I was comforted and ministered to even when I had no idea that God was working and loving on me through those beautiful ladies. Thanks be unto God! He sends people to help us in our time of need, to give us wisdom and guidance. I am blessed and forever grateful! As I continued to ponder more and more on why the Lord sent all those wonderful ladies my way, there was still that thought in the back of my mind, why did He allow Lady J to be a part of my life as well? I want to emphasize to you, my brother or sister, that we will experience a "wilderness" season at some point in life.

Roget's 21st Century Thesaurus describes "Wilderness" as **disorder, derangement, disarray, untidiness, irregularity, anomaly, anarchy, anarchism, disunion, discord, confusion, jumble, mess, muddle, hash, hedge podge, chaos, perplexity, labyrinth, jungle, raveling, entanglement, complication, convolution, turmoil, ferment, agitation, trouble, row, disturbance, convulsion, tumult, uproar, riot, rumpus, ruckus, scramble, fracas, melee, pandemonium, put out of order, out of place, desultory, anomalous, unsystematic, slovenly, indiscriminate, violent, complicated, complex**... (Thomas Nelson Copywrite, 1992)

Can you find yourself in any of these words? Are you in your wilderness? It may be helpful to search some of these words specifically to find the meaning. The Lord speaks of the wilderness in Deuteronomy 8:2 KJV, which says, "And thou shalt remember all the ways which the LORD thy God led thee these forty years in the wilderness, to humble thee, and to prove (test) thee, to know (learn) what was in thine heart, whether thou wouldest keep His commandments, or no (not)."

I don't believe Lady J intended to treat me the way she did, I think she intended to provide and care for me to the best of her ability. I could have stayed angry about what happened in that house, but through my relationship with God, I came to understand the truth of what had taken place. Yes, I was put in what felt like a dry place, one that was void of love. Yes, I felt as if I was deserted in abandoned land, but I had to consider a few things.

NUMBER ONE

The book of Genesis, chapter twenty-two, talks about how Abraham took Isaac as a sacrifice to show whether he would truly surrender, commit, and do what God had told him to do. My mother sent my sisters and I in the care of others because she thought that we would be better off with someone else due to her lifestyle. If I or we had stayed with her, I don't know what worse things could have happened, maybe even death! Please don't misunderstand me; I'm not excusing my mother or taking light of what happened to me; I am just saying that God knows what it does and doesn't take us to build our faith in Him. The enemy did not want me to see the other side where joy, peace, love, acceptance, and safety resided in the likeness of my Safe Haven. It was a major struggle for me and a real battle. God knows how much each of us can handle in our lives. It's the fight He puts on the inside of us that needs to come out! There are seasons in our lives that are likened to a wilderness, and the things we go through will strengthen and enable us to keep going!

Number Two

The book of Exodus, chapter sixteen shares how the Israelites complained to Moses and God after being delivered from Egypt. They cried about wanting specific food to eat and that they would rather have died in Egypt and remained in bondage than to eat manna daily and be in the wilderness. Manna was a special food they were miraculously given by God. This food is described as a white substance resembling frost; it was formed into thin flakes and tasted like honey. The manna could also be described as a foreshadowing of Jesus Christ, who is the true bread from heaven, John 6:32, KJV. Meanwhile, I would not say that I was in that same situation as the Israelites, but I was truly in my own wilderness, and this is where I get happy; this is where I get full! Although they complained, it is recorded that God led them for forty years in the wilderness, they were not only able to eat manna in the midst of their wilderness, but their clothes and sandals never got worn out. (Deuteronomy 29:5)Seriously! I have to let you know that My God made sure I was provided for; I had a roof over my head, food to eat, and He gave me a "Safe Haven."

Number Three

In Exodus chapter thirty-two, Moses came down from the mountain after spending time with God only to find that the Israelites had created a golden calf (an idol they worshipped instead of God). They danced sensuously and engaged in sexual immorality, which was strictly forbidden in God's law. Because of their sins, God wanted to destroy them and raise up another nation through Moses. Instead, Moses interceded for Israel, acting as a mediator between the Lord and the people, earnestly interceding in order to turn away God's wrath and change His intentions to destroy them. This chapter reveals that God always answers the prayers of His faithful servants, and right here, I want to use this as an example of how my mother dropped me off with my "godparents" and then later with Lady J. She decided to live her own life apart from God, this could have been a place where her spirit had not come alive yet, and she could have died because of her disobedience to God; however, she wasn't saved yet.

I like to think of myself as an example of Moses, who stood in the gap for the Israelites. I, too, stood in the gap but for my mother, first praying that she would come back to get me so that we could be a family, but eventually changing my prayer to her getting saved instead. Israel was in a God-ordained wilderness to teach them to trust Him, and I believe He allowed some things for me to trust that He too would save my mother. I can only imagine what life must have been for my mother; I have no idea what she had to go through while in her own Egypt ***(Egypt represents a place of bondage in the Bible)*** and then in her own wilderness.

What amazes me the most is how Moses's prayers were so intense and sincere that they moved God to change His mind to destroy the people of Israel and bring redemption instead of judgment. Though God does not repent the same way a human does, He is free from fickleness and sin; it lets me know that prayer indeed changes things. That's not to say that God will let everyone get away with their sins; it shows that He is a God who delights to be moved by the love, faith, and prayers of His faithful people!

NUMBER FOUR

Could it be that I was a catalyst in Lady J's life? Could it be that she was a catalyst in my life? Who knows what life would have been for us both had I not come into the picture? I never expected to live away from my mother, but had I been an answered prayer? When God created you and me, it was not in His plans for us to be abused, mistreated, molested, rejected (fill in the blank). It is a fact that those things did happen; however, it was no surprise to God. He sent His Son Jesus to take what the enemy meant for evil to turn those things for our good, and He factored them into His eternal plans! The seed was planted while I was young, but Jesus came to heal me and all those who need to overcome! Because he has healed me, I know Him as a healer! I know that He cares about what I (we) go through as well! I wonder if Lady J would have treated me differently if she saw me as a blessing? Everything that happened was not right, and God didn't see it as so, but He still had a pre-ordained plan despite all that took place!

God **knew** His plans for us both, and He was there every moment! No matter what we both endured, it was for our good! God had given all the women (Lady B, Lady C, Lady D, and even Lady J) in my life an assignment, and it was a two-edged sword for us all! Hebrew 4:12, KJV says, "For the word of God is a quick (living), and powerful, and sharper than any two-edged sword, piercing even to the dividing (division) asunder of soul and spirit, and of the joints and marrow, and is a discerner (able to judge) of the thoughts and intents of the heart." So, God was doing a spiritual surgery on all of us through His Word, which is living, active, piercing, and discerning! His word is sharp and two-edged, bringing healing and life to those who submit by faith; on the other hand, it pronounces judgment and explains the damages to all who disregard His Word, which is Truth.

Number Five

At times God will test His children. I had to understand that I needed to trust that God was there and that He had provided His Grace which was necessary for me to endure and overcome every circumstance that was within His Will. Let's look at what Jesus said in John 6:38 KJV, "For I came down from heaven, not to do Mine Own Will, but the Will of Him that sent Me. If you go down to John 6:40, Jesus also says, "And this is the Will of Him (God, My Father) that sent Me, that everyone which seeth the Son, and believeth on Him, may have everlasting life: and I Will raise him up at the last day." What I am seeing in this verse is, it is not the Will of the Father that any **BELIEVER** should fall from grace and be separated from God; neither is it His Will that any individual should perish or fail to come to the truth and not be Saved.

God is not going to overturn our ability to repent and believe. The blood of Jesus Christ was shed on the cross, and now everyone who believes in Him has the chance to repent of their sins. Although I was in my own wilderness and had sinned, I still had an opportunity to repent and do the Will of the Father. God said in Jeremiah 1:5 KJV, "Before I formed thee in the belly, I (God) knew thee; and before thou comest forth out of the womb I sanctified thee, and I ordained thee a prophet unto the nations." God knew me before I was created in my mother's womb, as we all have been. So, this tells me that I was also sent to do the Will of the Father and along with all those who believe His truth. Glory be to God!

God told me that He sent me to my grandmother because I would have gone in a direction opposite of His purpose and what Satan planned for me would have taken longer to overcome. I would have given up completely! It was not His Will that I suffer and hurt; God, Loves me! God not only told me who He sent, but that I too was sent because He has a purpose for me as well! All the distractions that were happening were to try and prevent me from seeing Satan's plans and fulfilling my God-ordained purpose!

As I sat there with all this going through my mind, I began to see how God intentionally and purposefully positioned different ones around me to stand in the gap for me. This could only be possible if they knew Him, which is why God sent me to my **"Safe Haven."** "He sent me where I needed to be, although some tried to destroy my life." He sent His Kingdom Ambassadors to come to my rescue! The Lord needed me to follow **His Word** as it is written so that I would be able to overcome what the enemy tried to throw up in my mind, like shame, guilt, rejection, and loneliness. He needed me to abide in Him so that He could abide in me to help others who shared my experiences make it into His Kingdom!

I went through so much, but **I still** had a reason to shout! **I still** had a reason to praise God! This is why I didn't view the church as a place to be entertained. There would be layers upon layers of bondages that would continue to be broken off of me, but this could only take place once I was ready to let it all go. God was the only one who could deliver me from these strongholds while I was on that floor, expressing to Him how sorry I was for all I had done despite what I had gone through. He gave me an understanding as to why I needed to repent. I participated in some things because of what happened to me as a child. I had turned to drinking, fornicating, and partying to fill those voids. I didn't know they were a cover-up until I started asking myself "why" I was doing what I was doing. I also needed to understand that I didn't have a pass to do these things because of what I experienced. I didn't have a pass to continue to give my temple to anyone other than my husband because God loves me, and my body was not just mine but His temple. Although I didn't have many partners because of my experience with sexual abuse, it wasn't about how many. I also realized how my past experiences were affecting my life. I was always suspicious of being in a relationship with a guy. I didn't hop from one relationship to the next because I didn't have the patience to deal with the many different personalities but to be honest with you, it was hard being with one person.

I messed up so many times, but I tried to learn from my mistakes the first time by living out the right biblical standards as I began understanding my worth as a young lady. By the time the Lord was finished with me, I had heard the Lord speak to my spirit and say, **"You can get up now; those people can't hurt you anymore."** When I heard that, my eyes were opened. I was also aware of my ability to have a say in who I allowed in my space. I had a say in who I allowed to put me down, and I could actually let them know that I had a Father who LOVES me! What He thought of me was more important than what others thought about me, and His thoughts towards me were not evil!

> ***"For I know the thoughts that I think toward you, saith The LORD, thoughts of peace, and not of evil, to give you an expected end."*** Jeremiah 29:11

I did not have to beg anyone to love me because the love I felt coming from God began to fill every void. His love is greater than any love I could have ever received or had been offered. As the Lord was speaking to me and I was receiving the words spoken, I can only describe it as one taking their first breath after they are born. God told me that He never left me, even during the times I was being abused and mistreated. He showed me how there was always someone there to protect me in some way or another. He always provided me with some form of comfort. I began to feel such a liberation that I had never felt before! At that moment, I began to praise God all over again! I asked God if He would please help me forgive every person I needed to forgive, and **He did just that, one by one!**

I was 23 years old when this mighty deliverance took place, but it wasn't until years later that I would be able to face Lady J. I believe God was letting me know that it was time to meet with her regarding the challenges I had endured. Well, as God would have it, Lady J asked someone we both knew to ask me if I could either give her a call or stop past her house after church. I decided I'd call her after service, and she asked if I would stop by her house for a few minutes so we could talk. I was very apprehensive about meeting with Lady J. She didn't indicate to me what she wanted to speak about, but I was curious as to why she reached out to me after all these years. I drove the 2 minutes it took to get to her house from the church as she still lived around the corner from my Safe Haven. I can't say what prompted Lady J to meet with me, but it was obvious that she needed to release her part in what had transpired between us over the years.

When I arrived at her house, I sat on the couch while she sat in a chair across from me. I couldn't remember the last time we had any interaction with each other; in fact, it had been about 8 or 9 years since I'd physically been in the presence of Lady J in her home. Although we attended the same church, after I moved out of her home and with my grandmother, I made it a point not to be in her presence. Whenever I saw her, I would turn in the opposite direction just to avoid us crossing paths, and now, I was in her home. As I sat there in a rather tense posture, I could see the seriousness on her face as she began by saying, "I called you over here because I wanted to say that I am sorry for whatever I did wrong to you and for the way that I treated you over the years." At some point in our conversation, she explained why she did some of the things she did. Lady J expressed that she and her companion, who I will call "Mr. Logan," was having issues on top of life happening, and I just happened to be the scapegoat she used to take out her frustration.

As she continued to confess, all I could hear was deep regret in her voice. I was so surprised to see her in this state because I have no recollection of ever seeing Lady J this vulnerable, at least not in front of me. On top of that, she started crying, and I had NEVER seen her cry the way I saw her cry that day. Then she asked, "Can you please forgive me?" Immediately after those words came out of her mouth, she bent forward and let out this cry that seemed to have come deep down out of her belly. Honestly, I didn't know what to do at first! I sat there for a few minutes; then, I got up from where I was sitting and slowly walked over and comforted her. I couldn't help it! I felt as if a heavyweight lifted off of my shoulders at that moment! I knew for sure that God heard my prayers! I always wondered and never understood what I had done that was so bad for her to act as harshly as she had towards me throughout the years. What Lady J shared with me that day confirmed a few things, and I experienced so much freedom! One, the mistakes I made as a child lacking maturity didn't warrant the treatment I received from her.

Now I knew the questions I had been asking God all those years! I stood there and couldn't hold back the tears; I was now crying along with Lady J! I accepted her apology while consoling her until she was able to calm down. I was in complete awe of God; I could not believe how humble she was! I also felt that Lady J was releasing years of her own pain and guilt for what had happened. By the time we were done, we shed what seemed like a pool of tears! Those tears held years of resentment, bitterness, and shame, but they were truly replaced with joy and relief! It was a true moment of reconciliation for us both! I would never have thought what was happening could take place! For years, my only focus and desire was to reunite with my mother and sisters; I never even considered that God just might have another plan for me.

"For my thoughts are not your thoughts, neither are your ways My ways," declares the LORD..." ISAIAH 55:8

I honestly don't believe Lady J expected to have this encounter either; this could only be God! It reminds me of Revelation 12:11, which says, "And they overcame him by the blood of the Lamb, and by the word of their testimony, and they loved not their lives unto the death." This scripture means that the faithful believers on earth overcame Satan by giving their testimony and were freed from the sting of death, by the blood of Jesus Christ, determining to speak for Christ, showing a willingness to serve Him at all costs! Over time, my relationship with Lady J developed into something beautiful. Throughout the years, she would call me, we'd talk for a while, and sometimes I would even visit her. She was a totally different person; she was calmer and easier to speak with. I was now in my adult years; I believed this helped me gain another perspective. I was also able to see her more vulnerable and sensitive side. I can honestly say that our relationship developed into a friendship.

What I came to understand was that hurt people hurt people, and sometimes it's the closest ones to them. Sometimes it's too late to make amends because there is no way to undo the damage that's been done, but it's never too late to make your wrongs right with others, whether they accept it or not. It's never too late to get right with God through repentance and asking Him for forgiveness for what you've done. Today, you would never know I had the experiences I did with Lady J, and she tells everyone that I am her daughter! So, if you asked me today if Lady J loves me, I can say this with no doubt in my mind and in complete confidence, **YES**!!!

Chapter Fourteen
Maturing And Answered Prayers

I was still struggling with trying to make ends meet, but eventually, I was able to get a job with another travel agency paying a little more than what I was earning. The only thing is the commute was 30 mins away in the opposite direction of my last job. Nevertheless, I'd gotten the hang of living on my own and keeping a routine. Not only was I experiencing a new life of being somewhat stable but independent. I met a guy who I will refer to as Mordecai. He and I met when we were both teenagers at my church. We both liked each other, but our friendship never really developed into anything serious due to certain circumstances. Mordecai had to go away and stay with some of his other family members, but after about five years, we reunited and got reacquainted. We still had some distance between us, but we tried our best to keep up with communicating. We talked on the phone and even wrote letters to one another until the day he asked me to marry him.

Sadly, our love story was short-lived; although I loved Mordecai, I was still dealing with hurt from my past, and because of this, our union did not last. Mordecai and I divorced, but I had my son Simba out of that union. He brought so much peace and joy to my life, especially in a time of so much uncertainty. I now had another person to look after, and it was not easy! Having my son was truly a humbling experience for me. After the divorce, Mordecai went his own way, I lost my job at the travel agency, and my car broke down again. Thankfully, my cousin Renee let me borrow one of her cars for a while, but I had to move in with my parents until I could get back on my feet. I got another job as a secretary in the emergency room at a hospital. I would now be working the night shift, but thankfully, mama kept Simba.

I learned some tough lessons during this time. I had many conversations with God about my attitude, character, and integrity. Also, I wouldn't say I liked being a young divorcee because I strongly believe in family staying together. I never wanted to bring a child into this world without having their father and mother raise them together, but I had to face the reality that this was now my life. This bothered me for a long time. Although I was still functioning at work, taking care of my baby, and going to church, I believe this sent me into a semi-depressive state, so I went into isolation outside of these activities. I was now back on the same street as when my grandmother took me in, only this time, I was now living with my mama and daddy. Remember the church I attended with my grandmother when I was younger? I would visit there whenever I didn't attend my church. I started working the night shift from 11 p.m. to 7 a.m., and I was still trying to get used to the work hours. My body wasn't trained to get up on time for church yet. I would go to whichever service my body would allow me to get up for. Lol, Some Sundays, I was too tired to make it to church at all. I continued with this pattern for about a year and a half. During this time, the order of things at my Safe Haven was changing. Everyone in my age bracket had gone their own way or were no longer members, but there were a good number of us who still attended.

I was in this routine of working, going home, and sleeping. Still, I decided that it was time to disrupt this cycle because it resulted from the many disappointments I was experiencing, even the ones I may have brought upon myself. I was finally going to give myself a chance to heal and move forward completely! I would try to go out with a co-worker and friend from time to time, maybe to a Christmas party or something like that. My mama tried to encourage me to go out on a date because I was still young. She said I needed to enjoy life a little more, so I went out on a date with a guy but found that we had absolutely nothing in common. After a couple of dates, I was completely turned off, and my biggest thing was, we had no conversations about God; it just wasn't working for me, and on top of that, I had no desire to date.

I didn't think I would meet the right person, plus my way of thinking was not the same as it was years prior. It wasn't like I was single with no kids; I was a single mother of one child, and because of my past, I was scared to allow anyone around Simba. It was bad enough that I had to overcome my own childhood traumas; I didn't want the same thing to happen to him. I didn't want different men in and out of his life. So yes, I was a young adult, and I needed to live and experience life, but I still needed to make wise choices. I needed to mature; after all, I was no longer living for myself; my love for God was increasing, and my relationship with Him was far more important. I didn't want to do anything that wasn't pleasing to the Lord.

In the course of trying to get my life in order, it seemed as if things took a turn for the worse, and I was being hit with different circumstances back-to-back that were beyond my control. I was in a car accident, and on top of that, living in my parents' house was becoming challenging. I was older, and I felt I needed space to live my life as I saw fit, and sometimes this can only happen when you're on your own. By this time, my cousin Ella and her son had come to stay with us, but we decided that maybe she and I should move in together and help one another out since we were both single mothers. So, we moved into our own place with our children. We did whatever it took to make life comfortable for the kids. In the meantime, I was still trying to figure out how I could get off early on Sunday mornings, go to church and come back home in enough time to take a nap so I would be well rested for my shift that night. I had sung in the choir and ushered for years; I don't believe there was ever a time I just sat in the pews. It was ok when I visited other churches, but it would be hard for me to sit in the pews at my own church. It was ingrained in me to do something for the Lord, but I simply couldn't make any commitments at the time. So, to get used to sitting in the audience, Lol I attended my grandmother's church.

Ella and I were still adjusting our schedule, but we decided to attend a friend of mine's wedding. My grandmothers' Pastor's wife was kind enough to watch Ella's one-month-old baby while we went to the wedding since the venue was near their home. We were halfway there when all of a sudden my car began to make this strange noise. I knew something was wrong, so I slowed down, pulled over on the side of the road, and called the Pastor's wife, and her husband came to our rescue. He (the Pastor) got my car towed, and we ended up staying overnight with their family; we never made it to my friend's wedding. After the mechanic looked at the car, he determined that it wasn't worth trying to fix it; I was going to need a new vehicle. With the help of Ella's friend, I was able to find the resources I needed to get a loan and purchase another car but how everything happened was simply divine!

Normally you go into a dealership, a salesman sits down with you, and they will pull up your credit to see how much you qualify for and how much your payments will be before looking for the vehicle you like. Well, because of the resource I received from Ella's friend, I never had to go through that process. The representative from the company I called took my information and all the proof they needed about my income etc. and faxed it to the dealership. They already knew how much I qualified for, along with my monthly payments. I only needed to accept their terms, and I would have a check mailed out by the next day via express delivery! I had never heard of this before, so I was hoping it wasn't some sort of scam! Lol Although I was assured that this was a legit company, I was still nervous; all I could think about was getting to the dealership and being turned down for some reason or another.

Ella went with me the day I went to look for a car, we got up early on a Saturday morning, and I was the first customer there on the lot. We were there for about 10 minutes when a saleswoman approached us. I told her that I was looking for a reliable vehicle that wasn't too expensive and didn't have to be fancy. She said ok as she pulled out the sales paper. We looked around but decided to go across the street to the backlot, and there it was! It was a nice teal mint green Toyota Corolla with zero mileage, and it was on sale for less than the amount of the check I had received! Of course, I asked to take it for a test drive, and before I knew it, I purchased my first car, brand spanking new!!! I had everything I needed, even for the insurance, and get this; I wasn't even at the dealership for more than an hour and a half! Because of how smoothly everything went, I felt that this was God's way of letting me know that He cared about my needs. I had been developing my relationship with God on a more intimate level; I had been praying more, reading more of the bible, and gaining more understanding of who He is. I learned to be more faithful to Him with my time, tithes, and heart towards Him. Now my focus was more on the things that pleased Him and my spiritual walk (how I lived). God was blessing me in a way I had never seen before, and no, this isn't just about the car, but how I received it. It was the grace I felt when I got the car! It's the way He pays attention to me, the love I feel when He does something for me, even when I feel like He didn't have to do it but does it anyway!

Despite all my wrongdoing, He is still there for me! It was truly a blessing from God, and I get overwhelmed every time I think about it. It was as if He was saving me all over again! Through this, God was reminding me that He has my back. Even through the purchase of a car, His presence was felt, and it let me know that He hears, sees, and knows me. Many other things in my life took place outside this that let me know God is real! This is why I want to stay in His presence and stay saved all the days of my life. I didn't want those desires I used to have because I felt something was missing. Again, this was not just about getting a new car my brother or sister; many loved me, but only God could and did do this for me!

He continuously **shewed** His love and kindness towards me! On top of all that, the promise God made to me all those years ago came to fruition! Remember all those years I cried out to God to save my mother; well, it finally came to pass! Over the years, God softened my heart towards my mother after I finally surrendered everything over to Him. I was no longer reserved or resentful; I was glad to hear her voice every time she called me. She gave me more details of what she had already shared with me about her past concerning the drugs, alcohol, men, and hitting rock bottom. I could now hear her out, and it was clear that had I lived with her, I probably would have been in a worse situation than I was in. The more we talked, the more accepting I became, which helped with forgiving her. Through these talks, the foundation of our relationship was rebuilt, but this time, it was stronger. We had come to a place where we could actually have a civilized conversation; she was different and not as offensive as she used to be. She was happier and now had good, honest, and loyal friends. My mother remained consistent with staying in touch with me and said, "I love you," more in the couple of years than I've heard anyone say to me over the 40 years I have lived!

I am Godly proud of my **Mother** for choosing God to help her overcome her struggles! She is still apologizing to this very day, but I have truly forgiven her! She now knows who she is in Christ Jesus; however, she has her own story to tell! God gave me understanding and caused me to have compassion for my mother because she also struggled growing up. She had gone through a lot to get to this place of Salvation. Now my mother is STRONG in the Lord! I am also proud to say that she has been clean now for over twenty-seven years and is an ordained Pastor!!!! Now THAT is something to celebrate over!!!

God totally restored our relationship!

Although I learned a lot about what my mother had gone through, she still didn't know the full extent of what I had gone through, but God gave me understanding, peace, confidence, joy, and love, which is everything a girl needs!!! Today, I can say that my mother is a mother to me and others (male and female) who lack the love and concern of their mother. God has given her a unique ability to articulate and display the love of God and teach those that desire to learn the Word of God. My brother or sister, who wouldn't want to serve the True God???!!! I was now feeling as if my life was turning around for the better! My relationship with God was on another level; he was revealing Himself to me more and more every day; with God's help, I was able to provide a roof over my and Simba's head. God blessed me to get a brand-new car, my spirit was more joyful than it had ever been, and I couldn't help but praise Him! I was still visiting my grandmothers' church at the time, and it was in the midst of worship that I felt a tugging in my spirit; it was God letting me know it was time for me to go back to my home church.

A couple of weeks later, I received a call from Lady B letting me know that the higher education department was planning a college seminar for the high school graduates. They were reaching out to college graduates to participate in a Q & A. She asked if I would come to our home church and be a guest on the panel. This was confirmation that I needed to return, and of course, I accepted. Although I got the nudge in my spirit to go back to my church, I didn't go immediately, but when I was finally making that step, the Lord revealed something else. It fell in my spirit that when I did go back, I would meet someone. I believe this was the purpose of my return. Now, during this time, I thought I was talking to myself and that I was producing those thoughts on my own. I still wasn't fully conscious of how the Holy Spirit operated back then. So, for the first time after a yearlong absence, I made it to the eleven o'clock service at my home church which was the same day I was to speak on the panel.

Right before I stepped into the sanctuary, I saw this man standing in front of the congregation, and at that moment,

I heard the sound of bells ringing in my ears going, DING! DING! DING! It was as if a light bulb had switched on in my mind and I immediately felt drawn to him! I walked inside and was greeted by an usher who seated me close to the front of the church. When I walked in, the man I saw was standing with the deacons while holding a basket to collect the offering. I sat there thinking to myself, "hmm, he sure looks familiar," but I could not remember where I had seen him before or if he was related to anyone I knew, but surely, there was something special about him. He looked like someone of importance. While I sat there trying to solve this mystery in my mind, the Lord also placed in my spirit that he was hurt before, and it would be hard for him to trust anyone. Now, I couldn't figure out why I even thought of all those things or why it was my concern?!

I couldn't get this man out of my thoughts, not even after getting home later that day! I literally couldn't sleep for two weeks, and I didn't understand why he was on my mind so heavily! I kept asking God, "What was so special about this man?! Why was he on my mind like this?" Was it because he was a new member? After all, I had not been to my church for at least a year. Well, I was now officially back home in my "Safe Haven," and I picked up where I left off. I continued dancing with the praise team. We would minister through dance to praise and worship songs. One Sunday, we had to minister through dance at another church. Meanwhile, our church was having a service about the same time, and since the other church wasn't far away and their program wouldn't be over any time soon, we went over to our service while waiting to dance. That was the day I discovered why this man was on my mind.

The praise team sat in the back of the church on the usher boards row so we wouldn't interrupt the service with our walking because we would have to leave out and return to the other church in a little while but there he was again. He was preparing to collect the offering. He began to speak with a deep, loud voice; he didn't even need a microphone! We could hear him clearly as he stood there holding the basket in his hands, asking the congregation to give their offering. During his request, he cracked a joke, and the entire church burst into laughter. He had a nice sense of humor. I laughed, but what was interesting was that night, I happened to sit next to his cousin on the usher board row.

Out of nowhere, she began to tell me the story of how he decided to give his life over to Christ, how he visited our church, became a member, and ended up on the deacon's board. In that split second, I knew then why this man had been on my mind. I took a deep breath because what came to my mind took me by surprise! I asked myself the question, "Am I interested in this man?!" Then I started talking to God, and I said to Him, "But God! That is a big dude! What am I supposed to do with that???!!!" Lol, quite a few questions were racing through my mind, but by this time, I had to head back to the other church to dance with the team.

That would not be the last conversation I would have with God about this man I could not stop thinking about, nor would seeing him in the front of the church be my only encounter with him. Later we would meet face to face. In my life, I would experience great joy and even more pain. So, you see, my brother or sister, my story does not end here; even with all I have shared with you, this is just the beginning.

There is more to be written...

Conclusion

My Hope

My brother or sister, I hope that in some way, what I have written thus far has been of help to you. You've only read a portion of my story, but you can still see how the Lord has been with me every step of the way! It took years to get to where I am now, and I now have peace concerning all that has happened in my life only because I surrendered what I could not handle on my own to God! I believe that if I had not let go of my past, the future that I am now walking in wouldn't even be possible.

In this book, I've only shared the first half of my life; as years went by, I continued to face more unseen trials and tribulations, but I needed to start here so you could see the whole picture. I needed to write this book so that you might gain an understanding of how life was for me in the beginning.

God continues to grow me as His servant for His Kingdom, but you will see throughout the chapters in the sequel to this book titled, "**The Cost of Standing while Staying**" how much I truly mature in Christ as well as how the enemy did his best to try and blind me from the purpose and plan God intended for me!

I truly give Glory and Honor to God! He has been my refuge my whole life. It was God who helped me overcome the many obstacles and challenges I faced! It was God who helped me to forgive! It is God who is helping me to grow more in Christ today and not let the cares of this world take hold of my mind!

Thank you for taking the time to read a portion of my testimony! Again, this book has allowed me some grieving and healing time as I had to go back and recall some of the things that took place, but it reminded me of my heart's desire which is to build a team of like-minded servants of God and to make our church a "Safe Haven" again. I know that God wants to do a new thing in our churches, and it starts within us! I believe God is looking for some true saints of God to help build His Kingdom. He is raising up an army, a remnant who are not seeking titles or to be seen, but who honestly and sincerely want to do the will of God.

There are so many hurting people out there in this world we live in. The enemy wants to use every opportunity he can to take out anyone who doesn't know who they are in Christ before they can come into the knowledge of Him. For this reason, I am willing to take time out for others that need a listening ear. I hope and pray that I can help those struggling in their own lives, those who have yet to recognize who they are in Christ as well as those who've found themselves in a backslidden state and want to find their way back to God.

God showed me Himself through His saints, and He used many different avenues throughout my life to protect me. Today, not only am I still a member of that church, but I am now the wife of a Pastor in that very same "Safe Haven." Only GOD knew the outcome of my life when He beckoned me to join my "Safe Haven" as a young girl.

Whatever you may be facing or need to overcome, remember this truth, God is no respecter of persons; what He did for me, surely, He can do for you. **Only Believe!**

By the Grace of God, to be continued…

About The Author

Yavon Smith obtained a degree in Theology and is currently studying to receive her bachelor's degree in Christian Counseling. She is partnered with an organization called, "Rise Above Defeat."

Yavon serves as a Christian Life Coach and operates as a Deliverance Minister, whose primary focus is helping others tear down spiritual strongholds in their life through the power of the Holy Spirit.

She stands on the scripture in 1 John 5:4, which speaks on the truth that believers can overcome their struggles with the past, habits, and addictions because "everyone born of God overcomes the world."

Yavon is truly passionate about nurturing the youth and imparting into young adults and the elderly to evoke transformative change. Most importantly, she seeks to serve God in whatever capacity He desires her to so that His name can be magnified and glorified.

Contact

To reach Yavon for booking, coaching services, or to share how her story has blessed you, please send an email to AuthorYavonSmith@hotmail.com.

Are you on social media? Connect with her on Instagram @authoryavonsmith and find her on Facebook, Author Yavon Smith.

www.ingramcontent.com/pod-product-compliance
Lightning Source LLC
Chambersburg PA
CBHW070506100426
42743CB00010B/1776